An Outdoor Family Guide to

ROCKY MOUNTAIN

NATIONAL PARK

SECOND EDITION

An Outdoor Family Guide to

ROCKY MOUNTAIN

NATIONAL PARK

SECOND EDITION

Lisa Gollin Evans

THE
MOUNTAINEERS

Published by
The Mountaineers
1001 SW Klickitat Way, Suite 201
Seattle, WA 98134

First edition 1991. Second edition: first printing 1998, second printing 1999

Published simultaneously in Great Britain by Cordee, 3a DeMontfort Street, Leicester, England, LE1 7HD

Manufactured in Canada

Edited by Paula Thurman
Maps by Jerry Painter
All photographs by the author, unless otherwise noted
Cover design by Watson Graphics
Book design by Bridget Culligan
Layout by Jacqulyn Weber
Chapter opener art by Catlin Culligan McNamara
Cover photograph: *Nymph Lake*
Frontispiece: *Sprague Lake Trail*

Library of Congress Cataloging-in-Publication Data
Evans, Lisa Gollin, 1956–
    An outdoor family guide to Rocky Mountain National Park / Lisa
Gollin Evans. — 2nd ed.
        p.   cm.
    Rev. ed. of: Rocky Mountain National Park. c1991.
    Includes bibliographical references (p. 232) and index.
    ISBN 0-89886-546-8
    1. Hiking—Colorado—Rocky Mountain National Park—Guidebooks.
2. Outdoor recreation—Colorado—Rocky Mountain National Park—
Guidebooks. 3. Family recreation—Colorado—Rocky Mountain
National Park—Guidebooks. 4. Trails—Colorado—Rocky Mountain
National Park—Guidebooks. I. Evans, Lisa Gollin, 1956– Rocky Mountain
National Park. II. Title.
GV199.42.C62R6245 1998
917.88'690433—dc21   97-43535
                                                              CIP

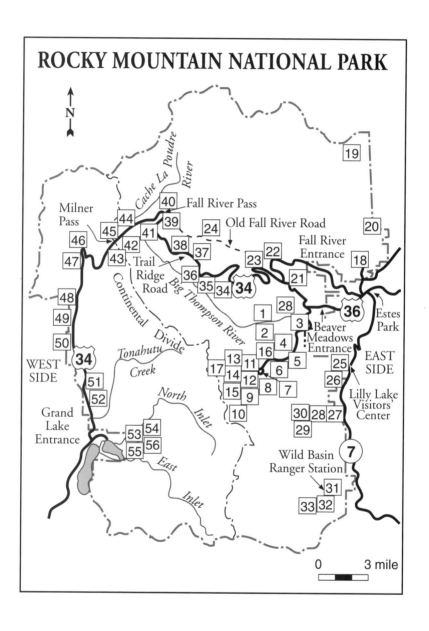

ROCKY MOUNTAIN NATIONAL PARK

N

19

20

Milner Pass

40 Fall River Pass

44
45
46
47

39

24 Old Fall River Road

38
42
43 Trail Ridge Road

37

41

Fall River Entrance

18

23 22

36
35 34 34

21

Big Thompson River

Continental Divide

1 28

3

36 Estes Park

2

Beaver Meadows Entrance

Tonahutu Creek

17

13 11
14 12
15

16

4

5

6
8 7

25

26

EAST SIDE

Lilly Lake Visitors' Center

WEST SIDE

34

51
52

10

30 28 27
29

North Inlet

Grand Lake Entrance

53 54
55 56

Wild Basin Ranger Station

7

East Inlet

31
33 32

0   3 mile

To my mother, with love
—LGE

LEGEND

••••••	Hiking route	🌲	Picnic area
♿	Wheelchair accessible	⌒	Bridge
♿*	Wheelchair accessible with assistance	▲	Campsite
T	Trailhead	⌷	Viewpoint
P	Parking	–(34)–	US highway
🚐	Shuttle bus stop	–(36)–	State highway
— ·· — · —	Park boundary	– – – –	Secondary trail
⋀	Peak		Rivers and lakes

Contents

Preface

The purpose of this book is to make your visit to Rocky Mountain National Park a safe, rewarding, and immensely enjoyable experience by showing you the best places to hike, picnic, find wildlife, and learn about the park's unique wildness. This guidebook is particularly meant for those of you who enjoyed hiking before you had children and who still crave the escape back to nature. You have chosen the right place. Rocky Mountain National Park is an excellent park for family outdoor adventures, offering an extraordinary variety of recreational and educational activities in a stunningly beautiful setting. With a little creativity and planning, your visit can be an invaluable introduction for your children to the beauty of nature and the importance of preserving wilderness. This second edition of *Rocky Mountain National Park: An Outdoor Family Guide* provides the essential information to make your trip the best it can be.

The key to enjoying your vacation at Rocky Mountain National Park is to realize that, with children along, your wilderness experience is going to be radically changed. This does not mean you have to succumb immediately to the water slides, bumper cars, and miniature golf concessions that lie outside the park. Nevertheless, traveling with children limits the scope of your activities, requires substantial planning for each outing, and demands a significant outlay of parental energy to ensure that your children's needs are satisfied.

Even so, your trip to Rocky Mountain National Park can be an enlightening and renewing experience that rejuvenates your senses and strengthens your family bonds. When hiking with children, you can experience the familiar woods, streams, and forest creatures in ways you had long forgotten. If you are attuned to your children's experiences, even your short walks can be wonderful adventures. The best way to make sure your vacation at Rocky Mountain National Park is fun for both you and your children is to approach your visit with open-mindedness and a childlike sense of wonder. If you do, your trip will be a joyful experience for the whole family, one that will bring you back—with your children—to the wilderness for years to come.

Acknowledgments

This book could not have been possible without the invaluable help of several good friends: Lisa Ferreira Evans, Richard Foote, Mary Ann Fomunyoh, Ned and Julie Strong, and Gennie Devaud. I also want to thank the former Chief Park Naturalist of Rocky Mountain National Park, Jim Mack, and the park service staff, including Douglas Caldwell and Dr. D. Ferrel Atkins for their helpful suggestions. In addition, I appreciate the help given to me by Curt Buchholz of the Rocky Mountain Nature Association, including Curt Buchholtz and Deanna Ochs. I also want to thank the staff at the YMCA of the Rockies, Estes Park, for their help in finding near-perfect accommodations.

I thank Kent and Donna Dannen for their fine and informative books, which helped me get started on this project. This book was inspired by the writing excellence of my brother, Jim, and made possible by the unwavering support of my mother and father.

Finally, this book could not have been written without the encouragement and incredible support of my husband, Frank, and the cooperation and joyful participation of my daughters, Sarah and Grace. Special thanks are also due to my mother who helped so willingly and generously with the revised edition of this book and to Grace who was an excellent hiking companion. Last but not least, I want to thank Martha Lovejoy for her superbly patient, skillful, and gentle care of my newest addition, Lily (who, for her part, also did her sweet best to cooperate). Thank you all.

Introduction

This book describes 56 hikes in Colorado's Rocky Mountain National Park. The hikes are divided into three groups—East Side, West Side, and Trail Ridge—according to their location within the park (see map on page 15). East side hikes lie east of the Continental Divide, which bisects the park north and south. West side hikes are west of the Divide. Trail Ridge hikes occur on the high plateau of Trail Ridge, which spans the Divide.

How to Use This Book

The hikes are classified as easy, moderate, or strenuous, according to their length, starting elevation, elevation gain, and terrain. Generally, easy hikes are 0.5 to 1.8 miles one way; moderate hikes are 1.8 to 3 miles; and strenuous hikes are over 3 miles. Because these ratings are both general and subjective, consult the detailed hike descriptions for specific information about trail conditions.

This guidebook also recognizes an additional category of trails called nature strolls. Nature strolls are short, easy, often surfaced trails, 0.25 to 1.25 miles one way, which can be hiked with strollers or wheelchairs (with assistance). Nature strolls that conform to federal standards of accessibility are so noted. Chapter 1 also lists picnic areas that are convenient to very short trails.

The trail descriptions do not provide estimates of walking time. Hikers, especially children, walk at such variable speeds that such approximations would not be reliable. To estimate roughly the time required for a hike, use the average walking rate of 2 miles per hour on level ground for adults carrying packs, plus 1 hour for each 1,000 feet of elevation gained. Rough terrain and hiking children obviously increase the time needed. After a few hikes, you will find that you can work out estimates for your own family. Very broadly, strenuous hikes require a full day; moderate hikes, a half day; and easy hikes and nature strolls, 1 to 3 hours.

Many of the trail descriptions conclude with a section titled "Hike Options," which contains suggested extensions to the featured hike. Often the section describes side trips of interest or tells how to link up with other trails to make longer hikes.

To help you quickly choose a hike that fits your needs, Appendix A contains a trip matrix that concisely lists for each hike information such as difficulty, distance, elevation gain, and attractions.

Appendix B indicates what animals you are likely to see in Rocky Mountain National Park, on which trails you can expect to find them, and the season and time of day they are most often seen.

This book also includes a recommended reading list (Appendix C) that contains numerous books on nature for children and their parents.

Hiking Tips

The following hiking tips will help you and your children make the most of your time on the trails.

Choosing the Right Hike

Hiking a trail that's too difficult for your children is sure to lead to frustration for all. Read trail descriptions carefully to find hikes that match your children's abilities. If you are uncertain how far they can walk, choose a hike that has intermediate points of interest so that you can shorten the hike if necessary. In addition, try to match a trail's attractions with your youngsters' interests, whether fishing, rock climbing, wildflowers, or wildlife.

The Right Time

The time of day you choose for your hike can determine the weather you encounter, how crowded the trail is, whether you see wildlife, and even the moods of your children. Take rhythms of the park, your youngsters, and yourself into account when planning a hike. Timing can be everything. For information on the park's weather and wildlife, see Chapter 1.

Snacks

Let hiking be a time when children can snack on their favorite foods. They will be working hard, and snacks high in carbohydrates and sugar are energy boosters. Offer salty snacks to replace salts lost through perspiration. Good-tasting treats can also be used as a motivating force for reaching the next rest stop. Also remember to bring plenty of water or juice, particularly in summer, when humidity is low and temperatures are high. Mild

Lake at Alluvial Fan (photo by Ned Strong)

dehydration causes crankiness in children, and more severe cases can cause extreme discomfort.

Motivation

There are numerous ways to motivate children to reach a destination. The promise of a picnic or a treat is enough for some children. For others, encouraging good-natured competition with siblings or peers does the trick. You can also give your children trail patches as rewards for completing particular trails. These small patches, which can be sewn onto jackets or backpacks, exist for most trails and are available from souvenir and outdoor shops in Estes Park and Grand Lake.

When a child's motivation wears thin, distraction can be the best solution. Hiking songs, trail activities, games, and stories often invigorate sluggish youngsters. Your creative energy, of course, must be high to convincingly engage your children. For some suggestions to get you started, see "Recommended Reading," at the end of this book.

Leaders

Allow the children to lead your group. When the novelty wears off, assign the leadership role to another. Rotate the job among your children, and you'll be amazed at the distance you can cover. For safety's sake, however, be sure children do not advance too far ahead or out of your sight and reach.

The Pace

As much as possible, let your children determine the hiking pace. You'll progress more slowly than you'd like, but the hike will be much more enjoyable. Adults will also benefit from slowing down: you may cover only half the distance, but you'll experience twice as much.

Positive Attitude

Praise your children for all their hiking achievements. Positive reinforcement for beginning hikers is essential and will build a solid base of good feelings about hiking. Refrain from criticism if your children disappoint you. Nagging and criticizing a child will not make him or her a better hiker.

The Right Stuff

You can bring along a variety of items in your backpack to keep children happy on the trail. Magnifying glasses, binoculars, bug bottles, sketchbooks, gold pans, or materials for making rubbings may provide welcome diversions for youngsters who need a break. For additional suggestions for simple trail activities, see "Recommended Reading," at the end of this book.

Young hiker at Bear Lake (Longs Peak in background)

Relax and Enjoy

When hiking with children, the joy is in the process of hiking, in the small achievements and discoveries of young hikers. Relax and enjoy. With children, you travel slowly enough to take joy in the sweet smell of the woods, the sweet taste of gorp, and the sweet squeals of delight from young, curious, and still-able-to-be-amazed children. With luck, you will find the child within you on the park's trails and be able to happily progress at "child speed."

Wilderness Ethics

During your stay at Rocky Mountain National Park, it is important to use the park in a conscientious and ethical manner. If you abide by the following rules and teach them by example to your children, the park will be a more enjoyable, wild, and beautiful place.

Make a Positive Impact

The rule of Positive Impact goes beyond the oft-repeated "Take only pictures, leave only footprints." It asks that you consciously attempt to leave the park a better place. For example, by picking up a piece of litter you enhance the beauty of the trail for the next hiker. Give children a small bag that can be stuffed into pockets for their own litter as well as for stray wrappers left by others. Parents should also be sure to carry their own litter bags.

A second way to create a positive impact is to set a good example by hiking joyfully, attentively, and considerately. Your model will be contagious. Just as a crowd gathers to look at a sight in which others are showing interest, so other visitors may follow your lead if you find a hike interesting, fun, or exhilarating.

Respect Other Hikers

Hiking parties with children are likely to travel more slowly than other groups. As a courtesy, parents should be aware of other hikers who wish to pass and should see that their children move aside to let them do so. Also, picnics and rest stops should be conducted off the trail so as not to obstruct the path.

Leaders should discourage excessive noise. Youngsters may readily lower their voices when they learn that noise scares away birds and animals. Children, of course, should not be expected to march silently, but neither should they make unnecessary noise.

Do Not Feed the Animals

Do not feed the numerous chipmunks, squirrels, and birds who beg for handouts at the park. Feeding can be dangerous for both you and the animals. Human handouts are detrimental to wildlife for two main reasons. First, snack foods nutritionally cannot replace an animal's natural diet. Therefore, if handouts become its primary source of food, the animal may become malnourished and prey to disease and injury. Second, feeding an animal disrupts its natural foraging instincts. As a result, animals who depend on human feeding may not survive the winter. After all, the animal that relies on cheese doodles in July is likely to expect them in February as well.

Feeding park animals can also be hazardous to people. No matter how cute the chipmunks and deer may be, they are *wild* animals, and wild animals bite. The park's small mammals, like those in many other parts of the West, have been found to carry rabies. Rabies aside, a rodent's sharp incisors in your finger is painful. Second, fleas carrying bubonic plague have been found on the park's rodents. Although rare, instances of human contraction of bubonic plague from flea bites have occurred in national parks. Finally, remember that feeding wildlife is prohibited by park regulations.

Often, well-meaning park visitors feed wildlife in order to get a closer look at the animals. For safer and more ethical ways of viewing wildlife, see Chapter 1.

Let Wildflowers Flourish

From June through August, a dazzling display of wildflowers graces Rocky Mountain National Park. During these same months over 3 million visitors pass through the park. To ensure that all visitors have an opportunity to enjoy the flowers, it is essential everyone refrain from picking even one blossom. Above treeline, picking wildflowers poses a particularly critical problem because alpine plants may not bloom every year and, even when they do, they have little time in which to set seed. Removing plants from any part of the park means removing seeds, thus preventing annuals from reproducing.

Picking wildflowers can be expensive as well. The fine for picking the Colorado state flower, the Rocky Mountain columbine, is $500. Because most wildflowers wilt quickly after being plucked, the crime is ill-rewarded in any event.

Stay on the Trail

The rule prohibiting shortcuts is essential for maintaining the integrity, beauty, and safety of the park's trails. Shortcuts are most tempting where a trail switchbacks down a steep slope. Yet these switchbacks have been cut in part to stabilize the trail. When hikers aim straight down a slope, they damage the vegetation between the switchbacks and contribute to erosion of the slope. If shortcutting occurs frequently, a trail may wash away, leaving a scarred and barren hillside. In addition, leaving a trail on a precipitous slope is not only dangerous but may cause you to lose the trail altogether.

As a related matter, do not enter areas closed by the National Park Service for "revegetation." Such areas have usually been badly trampled and need years of protection to recover. Respecting trampled areas is especially critical on the alpine tundra, where plant life is particularly prone to damage and revegetation is extremely slow.

Observe Park Rules

Written copies of park regulations are available at the visitor centers. The rules are also frequently posted on trails. Please read and follow them. A few of the most important—and most commonly violated—are the following:

- Carry out all refuse. Nothing should be left on trails or in campsites. You should not attempt to burn or bury noncombustibles.
- Build campfires only in designated sites and in grates if provided. Use dead and downed wood only. Never cut down living trees, or portions thereof, for your own use—not even for cooking hot dogs.
- Dogs, cats, and other pets are not permitted on trails or away from roads or parking areas. Where permitted, all pets must be leashed. Although it may be tempting to allow the family pet to accompany you on the trail, it is potentially hazardous for your pet and for park wildlife.
- Do not cut, remove, deface, or disturb any tree, shrub, wildflower, or other natural object. Wild edibles, such as berries, can be gathered in small quantities for personal consumption. Carving on trees is a harmful and unfortunately widespread practice. Carving scars trees permanently and can even kill them.
- Do not tease, molest, or feed wild animals. All hunting is prohibited. Observe the park's wildlife from a safe and respectful distance. You can induce great stress in animals by approaching too closely. Such stress can leave the animal susceptible to disease or injury, or can provoke it to harm you.
- Fishing in the park requires a Colorado fishing license for all persons 15 years of age or older. Check with a park ranger for areas of closure, possession limits, and restrictions on bait and tackle.

Enjoying the Park Safely

This section summarizes the basic precautions to be taken when hiking in the park. Be alert to the dangers described below and be prepared with the appropriate gear to minimize hazardous situations. The checklist at the end of this section lists the essentials that you need to take on *every* outing.

There are three important caveats to this section. First, it cannot replace a good first-aid book, of which there are many on the market. Second, neither the following information nor a first-aid book can substitute for a firm base of practical knowledge and experience in safe hiking and first aid. One way to sharpen your skills is to enroll in a first-aid course. The knowledge and experience you'll gain will be invaluable. Finally, safe hiking requires the exercise of caution and common sense. Know the limitations of your group and read the warning signs of trouble, including fatigue, stress, and bad weather.

Hypothermia

Hypothermia is the lowering of the body's core temperature to a degree sufficient to cause illness. The condition is always serious and sometimes fatal. Signs of mild hypothermia include complaints of cold, shivering, loss of coordination, and apathy. More severe hypothermia causes mental confusion, uncontrollable shivering, slurred speech, and a core temperature low enough to potentially cause permanent damage or death.

Because small bodies lose heat more rapidly than large ones, children are more vulnerable to hypothermia than adults. Early signs of hypothermia in children may be crankiness and fussiness, which can also be caused by ordinary fatigue. A child may not even realize he or she is cold until serious shivering begins.

Hikers, especially children, can become hypothermic when temperatures are well above freezing. Wind chill is a critical, and often overlooked, cause of hypothermia.

Parents can guard against dangerous chills by observing the following precautions:

- Carry an adequate supply of warm clothing, including wool sweaters, socks, gloves, and hats to insulate against heat loss. Gloves, hats, and scarves are particularly effective because they protect hands, heads, and necks—areas that are especially sensitive to heat loss. Carry these items even when the weather looks warm and sunny, especially when at or above treeline. On cool, rainy days, avoid cotton clothing, which is not warm when wet and wicks warmth away from the body.
- Dress in layers and remove unneeded layers to prevent excessive sweating, which lowers body temperature through evaporation. Parents must react quickly to temperature changes, whether occasioned by weather or changes in activity levels.
- Avoid excessive exposure to wind and rain. Carry rain gear on all hikes.
- Carry food high in carbohydrates and sugar that the body can quickly convert to heat.

- Carry warm liquids, such as hot cocoa, when hiking in cold weather.
- Avoid resting against ice, snow, or cold rocks, which draw heat away from the body. Place an insulating barrier, such as a foam pad, between hikers and cold surfaces.
- Cover the mouth with a wool scarf to warm air entering the lungs.

If a member of your group shows signs of hypothermia, stop whatever you are doing and take immediate steps to warm the person up. Promptness is particularly important when treating hypothermia in children. Add layers of clothing. Replace wet clothes with dry ones. If possible, administer warm liquids or food. If necessary, build a small fire to warm the victim and dry out wet clothing. Holding a cold child close to your body while wrapping a parka or blanket around the two of you is particularly effective. Crawling into a sleeping bag with the victim is recommended for cases that do not respond readily to other treatment.

Heat-Related Illness

Hiking at high altitudes, in warm weather, or in the open sun can cause excessive loss of water and salts (electrolytes). Failure to replace water and electrolytes can lead to dehydration, heat exhaustion, or even heat stroke. To prevent heat-related illnesses, consume adequate amounts of water and electrolytes. Avoid salt tablets in favor of salted snacks and liquids, which you should always carry in amounts greater than you are likely to need. Flavored powders containing electrolytes may be added to water to replace those lost through perspiration. Remember that thirst is not a reliable indicator of the need for water. Schedule regular water stops to prevent dehydration.

Sun Exposure

At Rocky Mountain National Park, precautions against overexposure to the sun are necessary year-round. Harmful ultraviolet radiation increases with altitude. Therefore, the danger is greatest at or above treeline, where incoming solar radiation is twice that of sea level. To avoid sunburn, take the following precautions:

- Protect exposed skin with sunscreen. Remember that children, especially babies, burn easily. Be particularly careful when carrying young children in back carriers, for their exposure may be prolonged and go undetected.

- Bring brimmed hats, long-sleeved shirts, and sunglasses.
- Don't be fooled by cool temperatures; you don't have to feel the sun on your skin to get a dangerous burn. Despite the frigid winds of the tundra, sunburns happen fast in the thin air.

Effects of High Altitude—Mountain Sickness

The decreased oxygen in the air at high altitudes can result in mountain sickness, whose symptoms include headaches, fatigue, loss of appetite, weakness and dull pain in muscles, shortness of breath, nausea, and rapid heartbeat. If ignored or left untreated, mountain sickness can be fatal. Consequently, do not overlook the early, easily treated symptoms of the disease. Mountain sickness strikes unpredictably. It affects both young and old, whether fit or not. Some members of a party may be affected while others are not. Some people may experience no symptoms on one day but quickly develop them on another. In any case, the cardinal rule when the early symptoms of mountain sickness strike is to descend at once to a lower elevation.

To reduce the likelihood of mountain sickness, acclimate your family to high altitudes gradually. The park ranges in elevation from 8,000 feet at Moraine Park to 12,000 feet on Trail Ridge Road. At the beginning of your visit, choose hikes in the lower elevations or, at least, those in the high country that are not strenuous. Because children are often inarticulate about their physical condition, be attuned to crankiness as a sign of altitude discomfort. If suspected, rest and retreat to lower elevations as soon as possible. Hikers with a history of heart, circulatory, or lung ailments need to be especially cautious and should check with their physicians prior to visiting the park. To aid the family's acclimation, make sure everyone eats lightly, drinks plenty of fluids, gets plenty of rest, and limits physical activity for the first few days. Adults should limit their intake of alcohol at high elevations.

Lightning

Deep blue skies and low humidity are typical throughout the summer and fall. Fine summer weather is interrupted almost daily, however, by early afternoon thunderstorms, which begin around one or two in the afternoon and last approximately an hour. Because of the real danger posed by lightning, plan your hikes so that you are below treeline by early afternoon. Start ascents or high-country hikes early in the morning so that you can reach your destination before noon—even earlier if your hikers are slow or you want more time on the summit. To be above treeline during an electrical storm is particularly dangerous because lightning strikes at the highest object in a landscape, which could well be you or your family in a treeless area.

If you do get caught in a thunderstorm, take the following precautions:

- Do *not* seek shelter under natural features, such as lone or tall trees, rock overhangs, or large boulders, which project above their surroundings. Such large, exposed objects are more likely to be hit by lightning because of their height.
- Do *not* lie flat on the ground. To do so is to increase the body area exposed to electrical current in the event of a nearby lightning strike.
- Do *not* seek shelter in a tent because its metal rods conduct electricity. For the same reason, do *not* wear a metal-frame backpack during a lightning storm.
- Do *not* remain on or next to a horse. Sitting on a horse increases your height; standing next to a horse gives the lightning a larger target.
- Keep away from puddles, streams, and other bodies of water, because water conducts electricity.
- Assume the safest position, which is to huddle on your knees with your head down. Crouch near medium-sized boulders, if available.
- If you are retreating to safety during a storm, stay as low as possible, remove children from back carriers, and walk with your legs wide apart.
- Safe places during thunderstorms include cars and large buildings (the larger, the better).

When hiking, be aware of the fickleness of mountain weather. Storms can approach extremely rapidly, turning blue skies to black in a matter of minutes. When hiking above treeline, continually check the skies for brewing storms. Although wind direction may be one indication of where a storm is heading, it is definitely not reliable. Mountains create their own wind pockets and weather systems. If you see a storm, the most prudent course is to retreat at once to a safe area.

Drinking Water

Always carry a lot of safe drinking water—at least a quart per person. It is *not* safe to drink from any of the lakes and streams

Enjoy the mallard ducks, but do not feed park animals.

in the park. The waters are often infested with *Giardia,* a parasite that wreaks havoc in the human digestive system. *Giardia* infestation is caused when mammals such as beavers and muskrats defecate in or near the water, or when water has been contaminated by careless disposal of human waste. Symptoms of giardiasis in humans include diarrhea, abdominal distention, gas, and cramps. The symptoms appear 7 to 10 days after infection. To purify water, boil it for 10 minutes. You may also disinfect the water chemically or by filtration, but these methods have not been proven as effective as heat. All water that might be swallowed must be treated, including water used for cooking, cleaning dishes, and brushing teeth.

To help prevent the spread of giardiasis and other harmful diseases, dig temporary latrines at least 8 inches deep and 200 feet away from water sources, trails, and campsites. Of course, hikers should wash hands thoroughly after use of the latrine. Parents should teach children safe toileting practices to protect their health and to keep lakes and rivers clean.

Snowfields and Icefields

Be extremely cautious when hiking over snow or ice. Never venture near the edge of snow or ice slopes or cornices. These areas can be treacherous and unstable. Do not venture out onto glaciers or glissade (slide) down snowfields unless accompanied by park personnel who are familiar with both the hazards and the terrain.

Streams and Waterfalls

The park's streams can be dangerous. The current of even small streams can be strong, especially in the spring and particularly for children. In all seasons, the park's waters are frigid and potentially hazardous. Flash flooding may occur during thunderstorms. If there is a storm upstream (even if it is not raining where you are), move away from a stream or canyon bottom to higher ground. Stream levels can rise extremely fast. Children fishing or playing on streambanks are particularly at risk.

Waterfalls can also present significant hazards. Slick rocks and steep drop-offs warrant a close watch on children.

Ticks

Rocky Mountain wood ticks pose a danger because they transmit a viral disease called Colorado tick fever. The virus transmitted by the tick is serious but rarely life-threatening. Symptoms include fever, headache, body aches, and rarely, a skin rash. Rocky Mountain wood ticks are active in the park from February until mid-July. A Rocky Mountain wood tick is about $\frac{1}{16}$ inch long, but may enlarge to $\frac{1}{2}$ inch when engorged. To prevent contracting Colorado tick fever, take the following precautions:

- Use an insect repellent containing DEET or permethrin; spray on shoes and clothing, especially socks, pant legs and cuffs, and shirt sleeves and cuffs. Avoid direct application of DEET to children's skin, for this potentially harmful chemical can be absorbed through the skin. DEET can also damage rayon, acetate, and spandex, but is safe on nylon, cotton, and wool. When buying DEET, choose a formula containing approximately 35 percent DEET. Tests have shown that this amount provides as much protection as formulas containing higher concentrations.
- Tuck pants into boots, and button cuffs and collars. Wear light-colored clothing to spot ticks more easily.
- Check frequently for ticks on skin, scalp, and clothing. This may be done on rest breaks while hiking. Ticks often spend many hours on a body before they transmit the virus, so there is no need to panic if you find a tick. Infection can, nevertheless, be transmitted soon after the tick attaches, so it is prudent to check regularly.
- Bathe after outings and inspect skin well.
- Avoid areas of heavy tick infestation in April, May, and June.

These areas include sunny south-facing slopes east of the Continental Divide, sagebrush clearings, and vegetation on the uphill side of trails.

If you should discover a tick, first cover the tick with oil or ointment to cut off its air supply. Then remove it using tweezers, as close to the skin as possible, pulling it straight out. It is important to remove all head and mouth parts to prevent infection. After removal, wash the area with soap and water. Even though ticks are rare in late summer and fall, you should still check your family regularly.

Rocky Mountain spotted fever can also be transmitted by ticks in Colorado, but it is very rare. Symptoms of this serious disease include fever, a spotted rash beginning on the extremities, headache, nausea, and aches in abdomen and muscles. Spotted fever can be fatal if untreated. Unlike Colorado tick fever, Rocky Mountain spotted fever is treatable with antibiotics. Therefore, if a member of your group contracts a tick-related disease, see a physician so that the appropriate method of treatment can be determined. No cases of Lyme disease, another tick-borne illness, have ever been reported in Rocky Mountain National Park.

Bears

There are no grizzly bears remaining in the park. A few black bears do remain, but their population numbered only about 35 to 40 in 1997. Although you are unlikely to see a bear during your park visit, you should still take the following precautions:

- Do not store food in your tent. Use a minimum of odorous food and seal it in clean wrapping material or airtight containers. Backcountry campers should hang their food in a tree at least 10 feet above the ground and 4 horizontal feet from the trunk of the tree. Car campers should carefully wrap their food and store it in the trunk of their vehicle. Ice chests are not bear-proof.
- When hiking in bear habitat, especially in brushy areas where your sight lines are obscured, make sufficient noise so that you don't inadvertently surprise a bear.
- If you encounter a bear, do not approach it. Bears are not usually aggressive, but they are unpredictable. Be particularly cautious if you see a sow with cubs. Never approach bear cubs; an angry mother bear will seldom be far away.

Mountain Lions

Mountain lions have been observed in Rocky Mountain National Park, and attacks, although very rare, have occurred. Although the likelihood of encountering a lion is very low, it is prudent to be aware of these potentially dangerous animals. Talk with your children about what to do if they see a lion, do not let them play outside unsupervised, and always keep them within sight and reach when hiking. Lions may be active at any time of day or night. Thus parents must be vigilant at all hours.

The Colorado Division of Wildlife suggests the following precautions:

• Hike in groups and make plenty of noise to reduce the chances of surprising a lion. Carry a walking stick; it can be used to ward off an attack. Make sure children are close to you and within your sight at all times.

• Do not approach a lion, especially one that is feeding or with kittens. Most mountain lions will try to avoid a confrontation. Give them a way to escape.

• Stay calm when you come upon a lion. Talk calmly yet firmly to it. Move slowly.

• If you encounter a lion, stop. Running may stimulate a lion's instinct to chase and attack. Face the lion and stand upright.

• Do all you can to appear larger. Raise your arms. Open your jacket. If you have small children, pick them up so they won't panic and run.

• If the lion behaves aggressively, throw stones, branches, or whatever you can get your hands on without crouching down or turning your back. Wave your arms slowly and speak firmly. What you want to do is convince the lion you are not prey and that you in fact may be a danger to the lion.

• Fight back if a lion attacks. Lions have been driven away by prey that fights back. Do not play dead!

• Contact a park ranger to report any lion activity.

Snakes

There are no poisonous snakes in Rocky Mountain National Park. The only snake inhabiting the park is a green garter snake, which is harmless.

Lost and Found

Carry current topographic maps for the areas in which you plan to hike. Visitor centers sell a variety of maps of the park.

USGS maps are particularly useful because they show terrain features and elevations by means of contour lines. If you have old maps, make sure they are up-to-date before setting out. Finally, buy waterproof maps, or carry the maps in a waterproof pouch.

Also carry a reliable compass and know how to use it in conjunction with your topographic maps. If you don't feel confident, check with outing clubs in your area for instruction.

Children are particularly vulnerable to getting lost and less able to care for themselves if they do. On a hike it is essential that children never stray from your sight. Take the following preventive measures to guard against potentially traumatic or dangerous situations:

- Teach children to stay with the group.
- Instruct children never to leave designated trails. Give children whistles, with strict instructions to use the whistles only when lost.
- Instruct children to remain in one place if they become lost. That way, they can be found more easily.
- If children must move while lost, teach them how to build "ducks" by placing a smaller stone on top of a larger stone. By leaving a trail of ducks, the children will be more easily found.

Special Gear for Children

The following gear can make your outings safer and more enjoyable.

Carriers

Small infants ride in front carriers; those able to support their heads graduate to back carriers. The best carriers on the market are large enough so a child has room to grow. Choose a well-padded carrier that has a storage compartment attached.

When hiking with a young child, it is good insurance to bring a back carrier, even though the child feels he has outgrown it. If the child becomes tired, the carrier will be invaluable. Carrying a child in a back carrier is much easier and safer than toting the child piggyback. Carriers can also be useful if quick evacuation from an area is required. For information on renting carriers, see Chapter 1.

Footwear

Lug-soled hiking boots, worn in and well fitting, are the best choice of footwear for children. These sturdy boots are essential for long hikes on rocky or steep terrain, or when children are carrying backpacks. The boots' stiff uppers and strong construction provide support and protect feet from injury. Before hiking, make sure waterproofing is fresh and effective.

Sturdy athletic shoes with good traction are a common substitute. Athletic shoes can be an adequate and comfortable substitute for boots on short outings and relatively easy, smooth trails. Athletic shoes give feet little support, however, on rough terrain. Also, if children are hiking in any type of sneakers, remember that the shoes are not waterproof and if soaked may result in cold, blistered feet.

Children should wear wool or wool-blend socks. If wool socks get wet, they will still keep feet warm. When hiking in cool weather, you may be tempted to wear heavier socks for warmth. If possible, wear two thinner pairs of socks instead of one thick pair—the layers provide more warmth. Always bring an extra pair of socks for each child. Mud puddles and streams are too attractive to be passed up by most youngsters. Extra wool socks can also be used as mittens.

Handicamp backcountry site at Sprague Lake

Clothing

Because of the changeable weather, always carry warm clothes and rain gear. Hypothermia can occur even in midsummer, and children are more susceptible than adults. Layers are the best for warmth. Carry extra wool sweaters and rain ponchos or waterproof jackets and rain pants. Before your trip, test all seams for watertight seals, and reseal if necessary. Sweatshirts are not recommended because they are useless when wet. In addition, carry hats and gloves for everyone.

Suggested First-Aid Kit

It is essential that you carry a first-aid kit on every outing. Once assembled, including the kit in your backpack will quickly become routine. Commercially packaged kits are available in convenient sizes, and some are quite good. If you wish to purchase one, check their contents against the following list and supplement when necessary. In addition, ask your family doctor to suggest medications that are specific to your family's needs. To make your own first-aid kit inexpensively, simply purchase the items listed below and place them in a nylon stuff bag, zippered container, or aluminum box. If size and weight are not problems, the box is recommended because it keeps supplies organized, so you can quickly tell when items need to be replenished. Your first-aid kit should include:

- Adhesive bandage strips. Bring many more than you actually need; their psychological value to children cannot be underestimated.
- Butterfly bandages for minor lacerations
- Sterile gauze pads (4 x 4 inches) for larger wounds
- Adhesive tape to attach dressings
- Roller gauze to attach dressings
- Antibiotic ointment to treat wounds and cuts
- Moleskin for blisters
- Triangle bandages for slings
- Athletic tape for multiple uses
- Children's pain reliever
- Adult pain reliever
- Betadine™ swabs (povidone iodine) for an antiseptic
- Alcohol pads to cleanse skin
- Elastic bandage for sprains
- Knife with scissors and tweezers. Tweezers are needed to remove ticks and splinters.

- Space blanket for emergency warmth
- First-aid instruction booklet

Remember that no matter how well stocked your first-aid kit is, the contents are worthless unless you know how to use them. A first-aid course will give you experience in using many of the above materials.

Checklist for Safe Hiking: The "Ten Plus" Essentials

Use the following checklist before departing on each of your hikes. It includes the list of "Ten Essentials" compiled by The Mountaineers and adds a few extra "essentials" specific to the needs of children and to the hazards of Rocky Mountain National Park. Bringing the following items prepares you for emergencies due to weather, injuries, or other unforeseen circumstances.

1. Extra clothing. The extra weight ensures against cold, cranky children and hypothermia.
2. Extra food and water. Extra food is useful as a hiking incentive and essential in emergencies or if a hike takes longer than anticipated.
3. Sunglasses. Hats with visors offer protection to youngsters too young to wear sunglasses.
4. Knife. A knife has multiple uses in emergency situations.
5. Firestarter candle or chemical fuel. In an emergency, you may need to make a fire for warmth or for signaling.
6. First-aid kit. See preceding list.
7. Matches in a waterproof container. The containers are available at most outdoor supply stores.
8. Flashlight. A flashlight will be needed to negotiate trails at night or prepare a camp at unexpected hours.
9. Map. Carry a current map in a waterproof case.
10. Compass. Know how to use it.
11. Protective sunscreen for adults and children. Test for skin sensitivity before the trip.
12. Whistles. These are to be used only in the event children become lost.
13. Water-purification tablets. The tablets ensure a source of emergency drinking water.

CHAPTER

1

Rocky Mountain National Park
An Overview

Rocky Mountain National Park covers 415 square miles and straddles 40 miles of the Continental Divide. Within the park, 20 peaks rise above 13,000 feet, including 14,255-foot Longs Peak, the highest summit in the park. More than 350 miles of trails for hikers of every age and ability explore montane meadows, lush forests, and treeless tundra. Over 150 lakes make fine hiking destinations. One of the park's most remarkable features is Trail Ridge Road, the highest continuous paved road in the United States, where one can drive above treeline for 11 breathtaking miles, offering easy access to vast expanses of spectacular alpine scenery.

Much of the park's dramatic topography was formed by alpine glaciers, which flowed downslope from accumulation basins high on the flanks of the mountains during the last Ice Age, about 10,000 years ago. By scouring canyon walls and carrying away the debris, massive tongues of ice widened narrow V-shaped river gorges into broad U-shaped valleys such as Forest Canyon, Spruce Canyon, and the Kawuneeche Valley. Glaciers in similar fashion steepened mountainsides, forming rugged precipitous peaks, like Longs Peak and the Keyboard of the Winds. Glaciers also scooped out the numerous depressions that now cradle the small lakes known as glacial tarns and transported the innumerable large boulders that litter the park. Known as glacial erratics, these boulders were carried miles by glaciers from their places of origin to their present resting places.

Rocky Mountain National Park is home to a large variety of plants, animals, and birds. Thousands of species of wildflowers bloom in the park each summer. More than 180 species of plants occur on the tundra alone. Over one-quarter of the park consists of alpine tundra, representing the largest area of protected tundra in the lower 48 states. Among the fascinating large mammals inhabiting the park's diverse environments are mule deer, wapiti (elk), bighorn sheep, and moose. Other wildlife to be observed include the marmot, pika, coyote, red-tailed hawk, and beaver. Black bears and mountain lions occur in the park but are rare and seldom seen.

The park runs one of the finest ranger programs in the national park system. Lectures, hikes, demonstrations, and campfire programs present numerous opportunities for children and adults to learn about the park's history, geology, plants, and wildlife. Well-educated and experienced rangers staff all five of the park's visitor centers.

Rocky Mountain National Park's proximity to Denver and other population centers, and its wealth of natural assets, make it a very popular place. Over 3 million visitors enter the park each year. Six hundred thousand hikers use the trails annually. The park has five large campgrounds, and it issues use permits for its 267 backcountry campsites.

How to Get There

Rocky Mountain National Park has three entrances, two on the east side of the park near the town of Estes Park and one on the west side near the town of Grand Lake. The east and west entrances are separated by the high peaks of the Continental Divide but connected by the awesome Trail Ridge Road. Estes Park (population 3,200) is the larger and more popular entrance, with more tourist accommodations and attractions. Grand Lake (population 500) is smaller, quieter, and more remote. The east side attracts more visitors, offering unparalleled views of the majestic Front Range Peaks as well as providing four of the park's five campgrounds. The west side also has superlative scenery, while lacking the east side's summer crowds.

Forest Canyon Pass in September, looking toward the Never Summer Range

By Car

Denver is located only 65 miles southeast of Estes Park, the east entrance of Rocky Mountain National Park. You have a choice of three possible routes to Estes Park:

1. The fastest and most direct route: From Denver, drive Interstate 25 north to US Highway 36, and then follow Highway 36 northwest through Boulder and Lyons to Estes Park. This route takes approximately 1.5 hours.
2. A slightly longer and more scenic alternative: Follow route 1 to Lyons, and then take Colorado Highway 7 west through Allenspark to Estes Park. This route takes approximately 1.75 hours.
3. The longest of the three routes is through "The Gateway of the Rockies": Follow Interstate 25 north to US Highway 34, and then turn west and follow US Highway 34 through the Big Thompson Canyon to Estes Park. The driving distance is approximately 80 miles.

Grand Lake and the west entrance of Rocky Mountain National Park are 98 miles from Denver. The drive takes approximately 2.25 hours. To get to Grand Lake, follow Interstate 70 west from Denver to where US Highway 40 branches north. Follow US Highway 40 to Granby and the junction with US Highway 34. Continue north on US Highway 34 to Grand Lake.

By Van

For van service from Denver (including Denver International Airport (DIA)) to Estes Park, contact Charles Tour and Travel Inc., P.O. Box 4373, Estes Park, CO 80507, (970) 586-5151 or 1-888-646-8687 or Emerald Taxi, (970) 586-1992, reservations (970) 586-1991.

For transportation from Denver (including DIA) to Grand Lake, contact Home James Transportation Services, (970) 726-5060 and 1-800-451-4844.

Reservations are required 24 hours in advance for shuttle service.

When to Go

Rocky Mountain National Park has much to offer year-round. Hiking is best from late spring through early fall, when access to park trails is greatest. The following seasonal summaries will help you plan your visit:

Spring (April and May)

In April, daytime temperatures (40 to 60 degrees Fahrenheit) permit comfortable hiking, but precipitation is high. Rain is likely at lower elevations, while snow still falls in the high country. All but the park's lowest trails are still snow-covered. Nighttime temperatures are cold, averaging 15 to 35 degrees. By late April, spring flowers begin to bloom at lower elevations.

In May the weather becomes a little warmer and much drier. Daytime temperatures range from 45 to 70 degrees. At night, temperatures fall to between 20 and 40 degrees. At lower elevations, there are generally brief daily showers in the late afternoon, which persist through August. May brings plentiful wildflowers, although snow generally continues to fall at the higher elevations. Usually in late May, Trail Ridge Road opens, making it possible to visit the tundra and the Alpine Visitor Center and to drive from one side of the park to the other. Depending upon the snow level, the Old Fall River Road occasionally also opens in late May, but heavy snows can delay its opening to early July.

Summer (June through August)

June ushers in superb hiking weather. The days are warm (55 to 80 degrees), but the nights are still chilly (25 to 45 degrees).

Wildflowers at lower elevations are magnificent. Brief afternoon thunderstorms are the norm.

July is even warmer, with daytime temperatures of 70 to 85 degrees and nighttime temperatures between 35 and 55 degrees. Snow still persists to mid-July on trails at the highest elevations. Wildflowers in the lower elevations are peaking in June to mid-July, while the tundra flowers bloom most spectacularly from late June to early July. Throughout July expect brief afternoon thunderstorms.

In August the average temperatures are the same as in July, but rainfall is almost double. Cloudy skies often replace the clear blue skies of June and July. Temperatures may fall considerably in late August.

Summer's warm weather brings the greatest influx of visitors. Park attendance in June, July, and August accounts for more than 60 percent of the year's visitors.

Fall (September through November)

Fall is a special time at the park. In mid-September the aspens turn gold and herds of elk descend to lower elevations for the mating season, which lasts into October. Clear blue skies prevail, and the hiking is excellent and uncrowded. The weather is brisk. Daytime temperatures average 55 to 75 degrees in September and 30 to 60 degrees in October. Nighttime temperatures average 30 to 40 degrees in September and 10 to 30 degrees in October.

In September, snow and rain may be mixed. The precipitation turns more consistently to snow in late October. Generally, the west side of the park receives more snow than the east side. Trail Ridge Road and Old Fall River Road may be closed intermittently in September because of snow. Both roads usually close for the entire season in October.

Winter (December through March)

In winter the park offers cross-country skiing, ice fishing, and snowshoeing. In this season, hiking is generally limited to trails below 8,700 feet elevation.

Where to Stay

Your choice of lodging sets the tone for your park visit. Camping allows you to make the most of your wilderness experience. A rustic cabin also offers a close-to-nature adventure, while

Aspen with bark bitten by elk

affording a minimum of modern conveniences. For all types of accommodations, it is wise to make reservations, especially during July and August.

Camping

Camping with children is both challenging and fun. Youngsters enjoy pitching a tent, gathering wood, and building a campfire. The tent may even be a focal point of play during the day, when a relaxing activity is needed. Camping in one of the park's campgrounds also gives you the opportunity to attend entertaining and educational evening campfire programs.

There are five drive-in campgrounds in the park: Aspen Glen, Longs Peak, Timber Creek, Moraine Park, and Glacier

Basin. Aspen Glen, Longs Peak (tents only), and Timber Creek campgrounds are first come, first served. Reservations are required at Moraine Park from Memorial Day to Labor Day and at Glacier Basin from early June to Labor Day. Reservations for summer camping can be made up to 5 months in advance by calling 1-800-365-2267. Reservations are highly advisable because campgrounds are often filled to capacity during the summer, especially in July. In June and September, park campgrounds are usually full on the weekends. From late May through September, camping is limited to 7 days parkwide (3 nights at Longs Peak). Internet reservations can be made at http://reservations.nps.gov/.

Park campgrounds are equipped with piped cold water and toilets, but there are no showers. Public showers are available in Estes Park. Recreational vehicles are allowed in all campgrounds except Longs Peak, but no hook-ups are available. Pets are allowed but must be kept leashed at all times. Moraine Park, Timber Creek, and Longs Peak campgrounds are open year-round, but the water is turned off in the winter.

To minimize driving, choose a campground near the area where you plan to hike:

- Glacier Basin Campground (152 sites): offers easy access to the beautiful Bear Lake/Glacier Gorge hiking areas on the east side of the park and is perhaps the most scenic of the park's campgrounds.
- Moraine Park Campground (247 sites): within easy driving distance of Estes Park, offers easy access to the popular Moraine Park trails, as well as to Bear Lake and Glacier Gorge.
- Aspen Glen Campground (54 sites): the closest campground to Estes Park, but not as convenient as other campgrounds to east-side trails.
- Longs Peak Campground (26 tent sites): at the southeast edge of the park; offers the easiest access to dramatic Longs Peak and secluded Wild Basin trails.
- Timber Creek Campground (100 sites): centrally located on the park's west side; offers convenient access to west-side trails and is slightly closer than eastside campgrounds to the spectacular Trail Ridge hikes.

Owing to the fragility of the tundra and the severity of the weather, there are no campgrounds on Trail Ridge.

Backcountry Camping

Rocky Mountain National Park offers 267 backcountry sites, including 35 sites less than three miles from the trailhead. Many of these campsites are identified in the hike descriptions. (For easy reference to backcountry sites, use the Hike Finder, Appendix A.) To plan a camping trip in the backcountry of Rocky Mountain National Park, call or write the park to receive the "Backcountry Camping Guide."

All users of the park's backcountry **must** obtain a Backcountry Use Permit. Campers can pick up a permit at the Park Headquarters Backcountry Office or at the Kawuneeche Visitor Center. Day-of-trip permits may be obtained in person year-round. Campers may also make reservations by mail or in person any time after March 1 for a permit for that calendar year. You may also make reservations by phone from March 1 to May 15 and any time after October 1 for a permit for that calendar year. For permits, write Backcountry Permits, Rocky Mountain National Park, Estes Park, CO 80517 or call (970) 586-1242. For all reservations, include the following information: (1) name, address, and zip code, (2) the dates you plan to enter and leave the backcountry, (3) the number of people in your party (limit of 7 per party for individual campsites and limit of 12 for group campsites), and (4) an itinerary with dates corresponding to campsites where you plan to stay. Backcountry camping is limited to a total of 7 nights between June 1 and September 30 and 15 additional nights between October 1 and May 31.

During the summer, campers with reservations must pick up the permit by 10:00 A.M. on the first day of the planned backcountry stay or the permit will be canceled in its entirety and given to other backpackers.

Camping Outside Rocky Mountain National Park

Additional camping opportunities are available in Roosevelt National Forest, which borders Rocky Mountain National Park on the east; Arapaho National Forest, which borders the park on the west; and the Arapaho National Recreation Area, at Grand Lake. For information, contact the U.S. Forest Service, 148 Remington Street, Fort Collins, CO 80524, (970) 498-2770. The local office, open mid-May through mid-November, is at 161 Second Street, Estes Park, CO 80517, (970) 586-3440. For the Arapaho National Recreation Area in Granby, call (970) 887-4100.

Several private campgrounds are also located near Estes Park and Grand Lake. For information, contact the Estes Park Chamber of Commerce or Grand Lake Central Reservations (see the following section for phone numbers).

Nearby Lodging

A wide variety of lodging options can be found at both the east and west entrances of the park, from plush resorts to rustic cabins, dude ranches to motels. Information on lodging may be obtained from the lodging referral service of the Estes Park Chamber of Commerce, Estes Park, CO, 1-800-443-7837 (1-800-44-ESTES); Estes Park Central Reservations, (970) 586-4237, 1-800-378-3775; the Grand Lake Chamber of Commerce, (970) 627-3402, 1-800-531-1019; and from Grand Lake Central Reservations, 1-800-462-LAKE (from outside Colorado), (970) 443-5391 (from Denver), or (970) 627-3324.

Unique family-oriented lodging is available at the YMCA of the Rockies, which has one facility in Estes Park and a second in Winter Park, near Grand Lake. Both YMCA facilities offer reasonably priced cabins and rooms, as well as a wide range of recreational and educational opportunities, including riding, swimming, youth camps, guided hikes, evening lectures, and concerts. For information, contact either YMCA of the Rockies, Estes Park Center, Estes Park, CO 80517, (970) 586-3341, or Snow Mountain Ranch, P.O. Box 169, Winter Park, CO 80482, (970) 887-2152.

Services

This section lists basic services available in and around Rocky Mountain National Park.

Groceries

Estes Park has two large supermarkets. Grand Lake has two small grocery stores. A larger store is located in Granby, 16 miles south of Grand Lake on US Highway 34. Groceries are not sold within Rocky Mountain National Park.

Outdoor Supplies

Stores selling camping gear and other outdoor supplies are located in Estes Park and Grand Lake.

Rental Equipment

In Estes Park, several stores offer equipment rentals with children's needs in mind:

- Back carriers: Colorado Wilderness Sports, 358 East Elkhorn Avenue, (970) 586-6548; Estes Park Rent-All, 1120 Manford Avenue, (970) 586-2158
- Strollers and car seats: Estes Park Rent-All (see Back carriers, above)
- Bicycles: Colorado Wilderness Sports (see Back carriers, above); Colorado Bicycling Adventures (downhill bike tours in Rocky Mountain National Park), 184 East Elkhorn Avenue, (970) 586-4241. (For more information on bicycling, see Mountain Biking later in this chapter.)

In Grand Lake, two stores offer rental equipment for children:

- Back carriers and baby strollers: Never Summer Mountain Products, 919 Grand Avenue, (970) 627-3642
- Bicycles: Rocky Mountain Sports, 711 Grand Avenue, (970) 627-8124

Emergency Medical Services

Emergency medical services are available in Rocky Mountain National Park, Estes Park, and Grand Lake.

Rocky Mountain National Park

Emergency phones are located throughout the park. In the event of an emergency, dial 911 or (970) 586-1399. For other assistance, dial (970) 586-1206. Emergency phones are available at the following locations: Bear Lake Parking Lot, Cow Creek Trailhead, Hidden Valley Ranger Station, Lawn Lake Trailhead, Longs Peak Ranger Station, and Wild Basin Ranger Station, as well as at all park visitor centers, including Park Headquarters, Alpine Visitor Center, Kawuneeche Visitor Center, Moraine Park Museum, and Lily Lake Visitor Center.

Estes Park

The Estes Park Medical Center, 555 Prospect Avenue, (970) 586-2317, is a full-service hospital with a 24-hour, fully staffed emergency room. Emergency transport by ambulance and helicopter is available. In an emergency, call 911.

Grand Lake

The Three Lakes Medical Clinic, 928 Grand Avenue, (970) 627-8166, dispenses basic medical services. Grand Lake also has emergency medical technicians on duty 24 hours a day. In an emergency, call (970) 627-3222 or 627-8244.

Picnicking

The park offers an infinite number of places to picnic. The following picnic areas are recommended because they offer parking, picnic tables, and uncrowded natural places for children to explore. All of the spots described below have minimal traffic noise and crowds, and all have paths leading to unique and lovely places. Areas accessible to the handicapped (with assistance) are noted, although access is usually not available to nearby trails.

For other picnicking ideas, check the Nature Strolls (NS) listed in the Hike Finder in Appendix A at the end of this book. Nature strolls are very short wheelchair- or stroller-accessible trails, many of which lead to wonderful picnic spots.

Bear Lake Road

On the east side of Bear Lake Road, from Tuxedo Park to Prospect Canyon, there are many excellent places to picnic. Each spot offers access to sparkling Glacier Creek, a view of glacier-studded peaks, and a buffer zone between picnickers and busy Bear Lake Road.

- Tuxedo Park: 2.8 miles south on Bear Lake Road from its junction with US Highway 36 (6.5 miles east of the Bear Lake Parking Area). Behind a quite ordinary picnic area, a trail leads down to five tables situated in a lovely, shady spot beside Glacier Creek. Flowered paths along the creek invite exploration.
- An A-Mazing Place: 4.7 miles south on Bear Lake Road from its junction with US Highway 36; 4.6 miles east of the Bear Lake Parking Area. This area offers a picnic table, fishing, ducks, and a maze of fishermen's trails.
- Glacier Creek #1: 5.4 miles south on Bear Lake Road from its junction with US Highway 36; 3.9 miles east of the Bear Lake Parking Area. This site features a shady table by a trail amid wildflowers and small boulders.
- Glacier Creek #2: 5.7 miles south on Bear Lake Road from its junction with US Highway 36; 3.6 miles east of the Bear Lake

Parking Area. This large, open, picnic area has three tables under tall pines, with a soft carpet of pine needles and a babbling creek.

• Prospect Canyon: 7.9 miles south on Bear Lake Road from its junction with US Highway 36; 1.4 miles east of the Bear Lake Parking Area. From a table on the edge of scenic Prospect Canyon, paths descend steeply to a fast-flowing creek.

Hollowell Park

Hollowell Park's expansive meadow and level trail (Hike 4) are perfect for children who like to explore. It is also a great place to watch for red-tailed hawks.

• Hollowell Park: 3.6 miles south on Bear Lake Road from its junction with US Highway 36; 5.7 miles east of the Bear Lake Parking Area (see directions to Hike 4). Numerous picnic tables are situated in an open area of sagebrush bordered by glacial moraines and large boulders for climbing. The site offers handicapped access (with assistance) and toilet facilities.

Moraine Park

The following picnic places are all in Moraine Park, which is located 1.5 miles from the Beaver Meadows Entrance Station on Bear Lake Road. Moraine Park is an excellent place for a summer picnic supper because it is a likely place to see deer and a wonderful place to view the sunset.

• Moraine Park View #1: 0.2 mile west on the road to Moraine Park Campground. A picnic table under a majestic ponderosa pine on the northern edge of Moraine Park provides good views of Longs Peak.

• Moraine Park View #2: 0.4 mile south of the Moraine Park Museum on Bear Lake Road (turn right to a parking area). These two tables at the east end of Moraine Park are located at the trailhead to Hike 3. The area offers handicapped access and good views of the Front Range.

• Fern Lake Trailhead: 0.7 mile west of the Cub Lake Trailhead; 0.3 mile east of the Fern Lake Trailhead (see directions to Hike 2). This site offers handicapped access (with assistance) to two tables located in a pretty spot rimmed by moraines and graced with a variety of trees and wildflowers. A path leads to the Big Thompson River and beaver workings.

Upper Beaver Meadows

From the Beaver Meadows Entrance Station, drive 0.7 mile on US Highway 36, and then turn west on a dirt road to a series of fine picnic sites, all with tables, grills, and handicapped access (with assistance).

- Old Ute Trail Trailhead: at the end of the unpaved road, 1.5 miles from US Highway 36. This is the best picnic area in Upper Beaver Meadows. Explore a creek, expansive meadows, an elk enclosure, and the Old Ute Trail. Toilet facilities are nearby.

Horseshoe Park

Located near the Fall River Entrance Station, these picnic areas offer excellent sunsets over Endovalley and a good chance at dawn or dusk of sighting deer in the summer and elk in the fall. After picnicking at any of the places listed below, explore the pebbly beaches of winding Fall River as it meanders through Horseshoe Park.

- Convict's Cabin Site: 1 mile west on Endovalley Road from US Highway 34 to the historical marker on the left. This site housed the convicts who helped build Old Fall River Road in 1913. Tables are scenically situated between two aspen groves, with a path leading to a lake. The area is particularly beautiful in the fall.
- Endovalley Aspens: on Endovalley Road 0.1 mile east of the Convict's Cabin Site. If the latter site is occupied, choose this one, which is similarly set among aspens.
- Endovalley Picnic Area: 2 miles from US Highway 34 on Endovalley Road. This very large and sometimes congested picnic area offers toilets, handicapped access, and 16 tables with grills. It also offers a stream and abundant birds and small mammals.

Deer Ridge Junction

This area makes a convenient stopping point when returning to the east side from a visit to Trail Ridge.

- Hidden Valley Creek: 1.5 miles west on US Highway 34 from Deer Ridge Junction (Deer Ridge Junction is 2.9 miles west on US Highway 36 from the Beaver Meadows Entrance Station). Tables and grills are situated in a scenic and shady spot beneath tall pines. The site also has handicapped access (with assistance) and toilets.

West Side

The west side of the park has many beautiful picnic areas. The four listed here are particularly nice. Sunset at the Kawuneeche Valley is a spectacular sight, as the sun sets behind the Never Summer Range. Elk are plentiful in spring, early summer, and fall. There is also a good chance of seeing deer in the evening throughout the summer.

- Lake Irene: 15.8 miles north of Grand Lake Entrance Station, or 5.2 miles southwest of Alpine Visitor Center on Trail Ridge Road. This site features a delightful high-country lake and a lovely easy path sprinkled with flowers and lined with spruce.
- Upper Kawuneeche Valley: 8.9 miles north of the Grand Lake Entrance Station on US Highway 34; 12.1 miles southwest of the Alpine Visitor Center. The tables at this very pretty wayside are scenically arranged under pines overlooking a beaver pond. The area offers good views of the Kawuneeche Valley and access to the pond. The site also features handicapped access (with assistance) and toilets.
- Coyote Valley Trail and Picnic Area: 5.3 miles north of the Grand Lake Entrance Station on US Highway 34. Adjacent to a handicapped accessible trail (Hike 50), this lovely and fully accessible picnic area offers expansive valley views near the majestic peaks of Baker Mountain and Green Knoll. The Coyote Valley trail swings close to the Colorado River and provides river exploring and fishing opportunities. Interpretive signs along the trail provide commentary on the history and ecology of the area.
- Harbison Picnic Area: 0.7 mile north of the Grand Lake Entrance Station on US Highway 34. From tables at the edge of the broad Kawuneeche Valley, enjoy good views of the Gore and Never Summer Ranges. This is a good place to see elk in spring and late fall.

Viewing Wildlife

You will see more wildlife in Rocky Mountain National Park if you know where, when, and how to look for it. The following section offers general principles of observing park wildlife. More specific information on locating certain types of animals can be found in the Wildlife Locator Chart in Appendix B.

Bull elk (wapiti) (photo courtesy National Park Service, Rocky Mountain National Park)

Where to Look

The best places to look for wildlife are where one type of habitat meets another, such as the transition area between forest and meadow. Such "edge environments" typically offer greater diversity of food and cover, and therefore support greater numbers and kinds of animals than either neighboring habitat by itself. The animal population of edge environments includes representatives of each bordering community, as well as species whose home is the edge environment itself. Areas that have a wealth of edge environments, such as patchy forests broken by meadows, or winding rivers with long shorelines, are productive areas for watching wildlife. Lush vegetation in these areas attracts large herbivores, such as deer, and small mammals, such as rabbits and mice, who in turn attract predators such as hawks, weasels, and coyotes.

To find a particular animal, you must know its habitat. In the course of a day, animals may use several different habitats for feeding, sleeping, hunting, and foraging. In addition, many animals change habitats seasonally. The more you know about a particular animal, the easier it will be to locate it.

When to Look

When looking for a specific animal, it is important to know when the animal is active. Animals may be diurnal (active during the day), nocturnal (active after dark), or crepuscular (active at sunrise and sunset), but in general the best time to observe wildlife is shortly after dawn or at dusk. At these times, diurnal, nocturnal, and crepuscular animals mingle in a transitional time zone. Furthermore, relatively few hikers are abroad at these hours, thereby increasing your chances of seeing wildlife. In contrast, at high noon in the summer, when human activity is at its peak, animals generally avoid the heat and activity, resting in day beds out of sight.

If you hike under the light of a bright moon, you may see the nocturnal animals of the park. Moonlit hikes can be magical and rewarding. Remember, however, that the use of artificial lights such as flashlights or headlights to view wildlife is disturbing to animals and is prohibited in the park.

Weather also affects animal behavior and, therefore, your opportunities to observe wildlife. Typically, animal activity increases immediately before or after a storm. Conversely, during periods of extreme weather, such as heat or cold, animals are likely to take cover. On windy days, when human scent is carried far, animals are more likely to be seen upwind than downwind.

How to Look

Anyone serious about viewing wildlife should invest in a pair of good binoculars. Decent binoculars are available for less than $100, although the finest cost several times that much. Binoculars make it possible to view an animal while staying far enough away so as not to disturb it. After all, most animals have acute senses and are likely to smell, hear, or see human intruders long before the humans see them.

For best results, tread lightly and dress conservatively. Walking slowly and quietly lowers the likelihood of being detected. Although most mammals are color-blind, birds are very sensitive to color. Camouflaging your appearance by wearing colors found in nature, such as tan, green, brown, and gray, will make you less conspicuous.

To further increase your chances of seeing wildlife, keep your eyes moving. Forests have many layers where animals make their homes. Look at the ground, the grasses, the shrubbery, the tree trunks, the treetops, and the sky. Look close and look far; your varying gaze is likely to catch something interesting.

When searching for animals, be alert to signs of their presence. If you can read the signs animals leave—their tracks, scat, feeding debris, nests, and burrows—you can deduce their movements and activities without actually seeing them. With a little knowledge of scat, for instance, you can determine if elk have frequented an area. By studying tracks, you can identify a fleeing animal and its pursuer, even though the drama may have ended hours ago. From impressions in the mud, you can see where a doe and twin fawns drank by a subalpine lake.

Finally, observe wildlife safely. Never approach wild animals. This precaution is particularly true for large mammals such as deer, elk, and black bear, but it applies as well to small creatures such as chipmunks. All animals can be dangerous if they feel threatened. For precautions regarding particular animals, see "Enjoying the Park Safely" in the Introduction.

Viewing Ethics

Watch wildlife briefly, respectfully, and unobtrusively. Remember that animals usually feel anxious around humans. If an animal shows signs of agitation, leave immediately. Most animals live in a precarious balance between the demands of survival and the costs of obtaining enough fuel to survive. Even short interruptions of an animal's normal routine, when multiplied by a park full of curious visitors, may have harmful effects.

If you find young animals, leave them alone and do not linger. They were probably not abandoned. More likely the mother is nearby. Your presence may stop her from returning or, in the case of bears, for example, may anger her enough to precipitate an attack. Furthermore, your scent on or near a nest might permanently cause a mother to abandon her young. Fawns and elk calves are routinely left in the forest while their mothers feed. The odorless and camouflaged young usually go undetected by predators. If you happen to find one, or any other young animal, marvel at the wonderful sight and then quickly and silently leave.

Finally, never feed wildlife. Feeding wildlife is dangerous for you and for the animals. It is also prohibited by Park Service regulations.

Wildlife Habitats of the Park

The park contains three distinct life zones corresponding to altitude. The zones are discernible as bands of distinctive vegetation, which is the key factor determining what kinds of wildlife are likely to be found in a particular area.

The Montane Zone occurs at 6,000 to 9,500 feet elevation. On sunny and dry south-facing slopes, the montane forest is relatively open and dominated by ponderosa pine. On moister, less exposed north-facing slopes, Douglas fir forms dense, dark green forests. Rivers and streams flow through montane parks that are carpeted with grasses and flowers. Their associated wetlands support willow and birch.

The ponderosa woodland, with its widely spaced trees and diverse cover of grasses, forbs, and shrubs, is home to a great variety of wildlife, including the most diverse bird population in the park. Mountain bluebirds, western tanagers, pygmy nuthatches, black-billed magpies, Steller's jays, and Clark's nutcrackers are typical. Mammals include Abert's squirrels, Nuttall's cottontails, porcupines, mountain lions, long-tailed weasels, and mule deer.

In contrast, the dense Douglas-fir forests of the montane zone choke out most understory plants and therefore support relatively little wildlife aside from the chickaree, a tree squirrel that thrives on fir cones.

In the open montane parks, coyotes and badgers find prime hunting ground for rodents such as the Wyoming ground squirrel and the western jumping mouse. In the meadows, elk and bighorn sheep find rich grazing and mineral deposits. Beaver and muskrat frequent riparian areas.

The Subalpine Zone occurs at approximately 9,500 to 11,500 feet elevation. Its forests are dominated by subalpine fir and Engelmann spruce. In disturbed areas, lodgepole pine and aspen are plentiful. On exposed ridges, limber pine replaces the less hardy trees. In the upper reaches of the subalpine zone, near treeline, stunted trees grow in twisted islands called *krummholz* woodland. Interspersed through the subalpine forests are meadows covered by sedges, grasses, and flowers. Wetlands border subalpine streams, rivers, lakes, and ponds.

The floor of the subalpine forest is covered with a variety of shrubby and herbaceous plants, which support a wide variety of wildlife. Most of the animal inhabitants, with the exception of the snowshoe hare, are not specific to the subalpine forest and can be found in adjacent life zones as well. As in the montane zone, streambank communities support beaver, which feed on the willows, alders, and aspens near the water's edge.

Birds of the subalpine forest include Clark's nutcrackers, gray-headed juncos, and ruby-crowned kinglets. Chipmunks and chickarees are among the common mammals.

Particularly rich in variety of wildlife are the so-called edge environments, where subalpine forest meets meadows, wetlands, or riparian areas. Here predators such as coyotes, weasels, black bears, foxes, and martens enjoy a wide assortment of prey, including northern pocket gophers, yellow-bellied marmots, shrews, and voles. Elk and mule deer are found throughout the subalpine zone, including in the *krummholz* woodland.

The Alpine Zone lies above treeline, which occurs at about 11,500 feet. The alpine zone features grasslands, meadows, low shrubby areas, and rocky fellfields—a mosaic of communities collectively known as tundra. Vegetation on the tundra must survive hurricane force winds, arctic temperatures, and an extremely short growing season. Animals inhabiting the alpine zone include pikas, yellow-bellied marmots, white-tailed ptarmigans, white-tailed jackrabbits, and northern pocket gophers. In the summer, rosy finches, water pipits, and horned larks are found. A variety of low alpine grasses, sedges, forbs, and woody perennials provide summer range for elk, deer, and bighorn sheep. One-third of the park's elk herd (estimated at approximately 3,500 parkwide) lives on the tundra year-round.

Other Activities in the Park

Rocky Mountain National Park offers a wide variety of activities for children, each of which helps them to learn about the park's natural environment.

Interpretive Programs

From June through September, the National Park Service staff runs an extraordinary program of guided walks, slide shows, campfire talks, and skill demonstrations. For example, a July day may offer a daybreak campfire breakfast, fishing and rock-climbing demonstrations, bird walks, sketch walks, puppet shows, photo walks, nature games, talks about mammals, tundra flowers, or Native American medicine, a twilight walk to see beaver, and a program of campfire songs and stories. The Park Service also offers half-day and full-day ranger-led hikes. A schedule of ranger programs is printed in the free park newspaper, *High Country Headlines*, and is available at all visitor centers.

The park also sponsors a Junior Ranger Program. Requirements include attending a park program, completing an activity booklet, and picking up litter. Children are awarded a Junior Ranger badge upon completion. Inquire at a visitor center for details.

Visitor Centers and Museums

The Park Service operates five visitor centers where friendly and well-informed rangers are available to answer questions regarding hiking, weather, directions, and other topics. The centers also offer an extensive array of books and maps for sale. Summer hours of operation are listed below.

"Meet the Mammals" wildlife program led by park ranger

Park Headquarters and Visitor Center. Located at the east entrance to the park at Beaver Meadows, on US Highway 36, 3 miles west of Estes Park, the Park Headquarters is open daily, year-round. The visitor center offers a short orientation film of the park. During the summer, evening programs are held nightly in its large indoor auditorium. For more information, write Park Headquarters, Rocky Mountain National Park, Estes Park, CO 80517 or call (970) 586-1206. Open 8:00 A.M. to 9:00 P.M.

Moraine Park Museum. Located at the east end of Moraine Park, on Bear Lake Road, 1.4 miles from the Beaver Meadows Entrance Station, this recently renovated museum offers hands-on exhibits depicting the park's geology and natural history. In addition, a self-guided trail pointing out common park plants is adjacent to the center. Open daily from May 1 through Labor Day, 9:00 A.M. to 5:00 P.M.

Alpine Visitor Center (AVC). Located on Trail Ridge Road, 20 miles from the Beaver Meadows Entrance Station, the AVC features exhibits on tundra plants and animals, a large observation deck over the Fall River Valley (where elk and deer may be seen with the aid of binoculars), and the world's highest puppet theater. Adjacent to the center is the paved Tundra Trail (Hike 40). The Fall River Store, also adjacent to the AVC, offers a variety of snacks and souvenirs. Open daily, June through September, 9:00 A.M. to 5:00 P.M.

Kawuneeche Visitor Center. Located on US Highway 34 at the west entrance to the park, this center maintains natural history exhibits and dispenses information about the park's west side. The center is open daily year-round, 8:00 A.M. to 6:00 P.M. through mid-June, 7:00 A.M. to 7:00 P.M. mid-June through Labor Day. For information, call (970) 627-3471.

Lily Lake Visitor Center. Located on State Highway 7, 7 miles south of Estes Park. Operated jointly by the National Park and the National Forest Services, this center provides information on activities in the park and adjacent national forest land and offers interactive natural history exhibits. Open daily June through September, 9:00 A.M. to 4:00 P.M.

Scenic Drives

Although the goal of this book is to get you and your children out of your car, there are two unique roads in the park that make fascinating and exciting scenic drives. Since both roads take you above treeline, be sure to bring warm clothes and sunscreen. Binoculars are also strongly recommended. Both roads lead to Fall River Pass, where you can visit the Alpine Visitor Center or get a snack at the Fall River Store (the only food concession in the park).

Trail Ridge Road. For spectacular alpine scenery, a drive on Trail Ridge Road is unsurpassed. The road climbs from montane parks through subalpine forest to above timberline, topping out at 12,183-foot Fall River Pass. Along the way, numerous overlooks reveal stunning views. The splendor of Trail Ridge Road culminates in 11 magnificent miles above treeline, offering expansive views over Forest Canyon and the Continental Divide. Before beginning the drive, stop at a visitor center for the "Trail Ridge Road Guide," a pamphlet that gives you a short history of the road and a brief description of each wayside. The round-trip distance from any park entrance is more than 40 miles. If you plan to stop at viewpoints, allow at least 3 hours for the drive. The best time for the trip is early in the morning or at dusk, when wildlife is likely to be more abundant than tour buses. Sunrises and sunsets are magnificent from Trail Ridge. Trail Ridge Road is usually open from late May until early October, although snow may close the road early and late in the season.

To reach Trail Ridge Road from the Beaver Meadows Entrance Station, drive 2.9 miles west on US Highway 36 to Deer Ridge Junction, and then bear left on US Highway 34, following the signs for Trail Ridge. From the Fall River Entrance Station, drive west on US Highway 34 to Deer Ridge Junction and turn right for Trail Ridge Road. From the Grand Lake Entrance Station, continue north on US Highway 34, which becomes Trail Ridge Road after Milner Pass. The Alpine Visitor Center is located roughly halfway along the route—20 miles from the Beaver Meadows Entrance Station and 21 miles from the Grand Lake Entrance.

Old Fall River Road. The unpaved Old Fall River Road goes from Horseshoe Park to Fall River Pass by a long series of steep and narrow switchbacks, rising 3,200 feet in 9.4 miles. Built in 1913–14, Old Fall River Road was the first road to the pass and the only one until the completion of Trail Ridge Road in 1932. Old Fall River Road is now maintained as a one-way scenic attraction. It offers an intimacy and a sense of history that is lost on the finely engineered Trail Ridge Road. No buses or trailers can attempt this route. Steep hairpin turns make the climb laboriously slow, but there are rich rewards for the additional effort. Drive the road at dawn or near sunset and you'll have it to yourself. Meadows in the upper sections are good places to see deer or elk at those hours. Be sure to pick up the booklet "The Old Fall River Road, Motor Nature Trail," which provides interesting information regarding the history of the road and its flora and fauna. The booklet is available at park visitor centers. Allow at least 3 hours round-trip for the drive to allow time for stopping at scenic viewpoints.

To reach Old Fall River Road from the Beaver Meadows Entrance Station, drive 2.9 miles east on US Highway 36 to Deer Ridge Junction. At the junction, turn right onto US Highway 34, heading north to Horseshoe Park. At 1.7 miles from Deer Ridge Junction, turn left at the sign for Endovalley and Old Fall River Road. From the Fall River Entrance Station, drive west on US Highway 34 to the Endovalley Road. Old Fall River Road begins after 2 miles, at the end of the paved road. Since Old Fall River Road is one-way, the return will be via Trail Ridge Road. Old Fall River Road is open from July until September, weather permitting.

Horseback Riding

Horseback riding is permitted on many of the trails in Rocky Mountain National Park. Guided rides are available from the riding concessions located at Moraine Park and Glacier Creek. The concessions offer rides ranging in length from 1 hour to a full day. Children under six generally ride with an adult for a reduced price. For more information, call Hi Country Stables at Glacier Creek, (970) 586-3244, or Moraine Park, (970) 586-2327.

In addition, a number of stables located outside the park in Grand Lake and Estes Park offer rides within the park. For a list of these stables, see "Activities Outside the Park" later in this chapter.

Fishing

Fishing is permitted in many of the lakes and streams in the park. Four species of trout can be found in park waters: rainbow, brook, German brown, and cutthroat. Although the park's waters generally yield only small fish, children of all ages enjoy the pastime.

Anglers should acquaint themselves with the many important regulations that have been enacted to ensure the survival of the park's native species of trout. The park's indigenous greenback cutthroat trout is threatened with extinction and has been placed on the Threatened Species list. Some lakes and streams, including Bear Lake, are closed to fishing to protect the threatened trout. Be sure to stop at a park visitor center to obtain a copy of the regulations governing possession limits, methods of capture, prohibited waters, and designated catch-and-release areas. Colorado fishing licenses are required for anglers over the age of 15.

The following lakes and their associated streams are among the better fishing spots in the park:

Sprague Lake (Hike 5)	Sky Pond (Hike 10)
Mills Lake (Hike 8)	Lake Haiyaha (Hike 15)
Loch Vale (Hike 9)	Lily Lake (Hike 26)
Lake of Glass (Hike 10)	Chasm Lake (Hike 29)

Guided fly-fishing excursions in Rocky Mountain National Park are offered by Scots Sporting Goods, 870 Moraine Avenue, Estes Park, (970) 586-2877 and Colorado Wilderness Sports, Inc., 358 East Elkhorn Avenue, Estes Park, (970) 586-6548, 1-800-504-6642. Both stores also rent equipment. To guarantee success for your youngest anglers, visit Trout Haven, where they can catch rainbows in a stocked pond and have them cooked to order at the pondside cafe. Located at 810 Moraine Avenue, Estes Park, (970) 586-5525. Peter's Pond also offers a guaranteed catch and grills on-site for picnics. Located at 510 Moraine Avenue, Estes Park, (970) 586-5171.

Rock Climbing

The park's rock-walled mountains and cliffs provide excellent opportunities for rock climbing. The most popular climbing area in the park is the south-facing cliffs of Lumpy Ridge, along the park's northeastern boundary. Portions of Lumpy Ridge have been temporarily closed to climbers and hikers, however, to provide a sanctuary for birds of prey whose populations have recently suffered a decline. If you are planning to visit the Lumpy Ridge area, please contact a park ranger for information regarding closure.

For climbing instruction, the Colorado Mountain School offers a youth climbing program for children age seven and older. The school offers both half-day and full-day climbs, including instruction in rope climbing and rappelling. The Colorado Mountain

Horseback riding near Glacier Creek

School is conveniently located just outside the park's eastern entrance in Estes Park. For more information, contact the Colorado Mountain School, 351 Moraine Avenue, Box 2062, Estes Park, CO 80517, (970) 586-5758 or 1-800-444-0730. Vertical Ventures at Colorado Wilderness Sports, Inc., also offers climbing instruction, equipment rental, and an indoor climbing gym. Special children's instruction is offered daily, as well as 3-day mini-camps. Located at 358 East Elkhorn Avenue, Estes Park, (970) 586-6548, 1-800-504-6642.

For visitors interested in watching climbers, take the hike to Chasm Lake (Hike 29). Watching the climbers on the sheer east face of Longs Peak is amazing and inspiring. Be sure to bring binoculars; the intrepid climbers may be hanging 2,000 vertical feet above you!

Activities Outside the Park

Rocky Mountain National Park does not have a monopoly on beautiful scenery or recreational resources. To add variety to your vacation, you may want to engage in activities such as rafting, mountain biking, and horseback riding outside the park boundaries. Museums and historical sites in and around Estes Park and

Grand Lake can also enrich your visit while providing a welcome change of pace.

Rafting

Rafting companies run trips on the Colorado and Poudre Rivers just outside Rocky Mountain National Park. The rafts are oar-powered and require riders to paddle. All trips require at least a half day. The minimum age allowed on the trips varies, depending on the class (degree of difficulty) of the river and on the policies of the particular rafting company. All age requirements noted below are subject to change. Parents must inquire specifically at the time of booking.

Colorado River Trips. Several companies offer trips down the Colorado River. The trip combines moderate rapids with stretches of peaceful floating. One- or two-day trips are available. The rafting site is about 45 minutes from Grand Lake and time on the river is estimated at 5 to 6 hours for each day of rafting. June and July are generally the best months to raft this river.

- Mad River Rafting, P.O. Box 650, Winter Park, CO 80482, (303) 726-5290 or 1-800-451-4844; minimum age: three years; shuttle provided from Grand Lake.
- Colorado Wilderness Sports, Inc., 358 East Elkhorn Avenue, Estes Park, CO 80517, (970) 586-6548 or 1-800-504-6642; minimum age: four years; shuttle provided from Granby.
- Rapid Transit Rafting, P.O. Box 4095, Estes Park, CO 80517, (970) 586-8852 or 1-800-367-8523; minimum age: three years; shuttle provided from Estes Park and Grand Lake.

Poudre River Trips. Two trips are offered on the Poudre River: one a peaceful float trip with some moderate rapids; the second a more demanding trip with difficult rapids. Full- and half-day trips are available. The drive from Estes Park to the rafting site takes about 1 hour, and time on the river for both trips is 2.5 to 3 hours. The concessionaires do not provide transportation to the rafting site. The best time to run the Poudre River is generally late May through June.

- Colorado Wilderness Sports, Inc., 358 East Elkhorn Avenue, Estes Park, CO 80517, (970) 586-6548 or 1-800-504-6642; minimum age: six and twelve depending on trip.
- A-1 Wildwater, Inc., 317 Stover Street, Fort Collins, CO 80524, (970) 224-3379, 1-800-369-4165; minimum age: eight and twelve years, depending on trip.

- Wanderlust, 3500 Bingham Hill, Fort Collins, CO 80521, (970) 484-1219, 1-800-745-7238; minimum age: seven years.

Horseback Riding

The following stables offer rides both inside and outside Rocky Mountain National Park.

Estes Park and Vicinity
- Sombrero Ranch, US Highway 34 East, Estes Park, CO 80517, (970) 586-4577
- Elkhorn Stables, 650 West Elkhorn Avenue, Estes Park, CO 80517, (970) 586-3291
- National Park Village Stables, US Highway 34, Estes Park, CO 80517, (970) 586-5269
- Cowpoke Corner Corral, State Highway 66, Estes Park, CO 80517, (303) 586-5890
- YMCA of the Rockies, Estes Park Center, 2515 Tunnel Road, Estes Park, CO 80517, (970) 586-3341
- Allenspark Stables, Allenspark, CO 80510 (303) 747-2551 (summer), (303) 442-0258
- Wild Basin Lodge, 1130 County Road 84 W, Allenspark, CO 80510, (303) 747-2552
- Glen Haven Livery, 7408 County Road 43, Glen Haven, CO 80532, (970) 586-2669

Grand Lake and Vicinity
- Winding River Resort Village, Grand Lake, CO 80447, (970) 627-3215
- Sombrero Ranch, Grand Lake, CO 80447, (970) 627-3514
- Broken Spur Ranch & Stables, Snow Mountain Ranch, YMCA of the Rockies, P.O. Box 169, Winter Park, CO 80482, (970) 887-2152

For a charming horse experience of a totally different sort, take the family on a handsome carriage ride around Estes Park. Contact Black Canyon Carriages, Inc., P.O. Box 6000, Estes Park, CO 80517, (970) 586-6696.

Mountain Biking

Bicycling on trails is prohibited in Rocky Mountain National Park, as is off-trail mountain biking. Mountain biking is permitted outside wilderness areas within the adjacent Roosevelt and Arapaho National Forests. Be forewarned that this is a demanding sport, appropriate only for older children. For more information, contact the National Forest office in Estes Park, (970) 586-3440.

Cycling enthusiasts may also choose to ride the park's demanding roads. Extreme caution, however, must be exercised when biking park roads owing to heavy traffic, narrow shoulders, and steep inclines. Early morning cycling is best because of reduced vehicular traffic. Mountain bikes may be rented from the following:

- Colorado Bicycling Adventures, 184 East Elkhorn Avenue, Estes Park, CO 80517, (303) 586-4241
- Rocky Mountain Sports, 711 Grand Avenue, Grand Lake, CO 80447, (970) 627-8124 (also rents bikes with attached child's seat)
- Aspen Lodge Ranch Resort, State Highway 7, Estes Park, (970) 586-8133

All stores offer bikes suitable for youngsters and provide maps with suggested trails.

Rainy Day Activities

Inclement weather, illness, or injury might keep you off the trails temporarily, but don't despair. There are interesting places to visit in Estes Park and Grand Lake that will please your youngsters and create new opportunities to learn about the ecology, geology, and history of the region.

In and Around Estes Park
- Estes Park Historical Museum, 200 Fourth Street at US Highway 36, Estes Park, CO 80517, (970) 586-6256. This museum will appeal to older youngsters who have an interest in Western history. There are amusing artifacts from the pioneer days, old photographs, an antique car, a homestead cabin, and an interactive children's area. Open daily May through September; Friday through Sunday, October through April.
- Dick's Rock Museum, 490 Moraine Route, Estes Park, CO 80517, (970) 586-4180. With lots of native treasures mixed with rocks, geodes, and crystals from all over the world, this "hands-on" museum/store is a rock lover's dream. Countless specimens are displayed at child level and can be inspected by

Golden-mantled ground squirrel (unlike a chipmunk, its stripes don't reach its face)

curious hands. One room shows visitors how rocks are cut and polished. Open daily. Admission free.

- MacGregor Ranch Museum, Devil's Gulch Road, Estes Park, CO 80517, (970) 586-3749. This museum is actually a homesteader's ranch that survives largely unchanged from the 1870s. Children may find the old ranch equipment interesting. Open Tuesday through Saturday, Memorial Day through Labor Day. Admission free.

- Eagle Plume Gallery and Museum of Native American Arts (10 miles south of Estes Park on Colorado State Highway 7), Box 447, Allenspark, CO 80510, (970) 586-4710. This museum and gallery houses a fascinating collection of Native American art and artifacts. Within the small store/museum are beautiful jewelry, rugs, pottery, and artifacts such as weapons, beaded infant carriers, robes, and headdresses. There is even a tepee, which may be entered and inspected by all. Open daily May 15 through September 15. Admission free.

- Enos Mills Homestead Cabin, Colorado State Highway 7 (8 miles south of Estes Park from the junction of US Highway 36 and Colorado State Highway 7). Enos Mills's log cabin, built in 1885, is lovingly preserved and filled with period photographs and artifacts. It is located at the end of a short nature trail. Mills was instrumental in the creation of Rocky Mountain National Park. Open daily. Admission free.

- Estes Park Public Library, 225 East Elkhorn Avenue, Estes Park, CO 80517, (970) 586-8116. This small library has a pleasant staff and a fine children's room with games and art supplies as well as books. Children's videos may be watched on the premises. If you are a regular visitor to Estes Park, you may obtain a seasonal library card. Open daily and many evenings.

In Grand Lake
- Kauffman House, 407 Pitkin, Grand Lake, CO 80447, (970) 627-8562. This log hotel was built in 1892. Now restored, it hosts a museum of local pioneer memorabilia. Open afternoons daily from June through August.

Special Events

A variety of special events are held in Estes Park and Grand Lake throughout the summer and fall. Some of the notable happenings include music and art festivals, horse shows and rodeos, bike races, and July Fourth fireworks. Check local papers and the Chamber of Commerce for information. In general, there is more activity in Estes Park than in the considerably smaller and quieter Grand Lake. If you want the season's schedule of events, write the chambers of commerce in Estes Park and Grand Lake at the following addresses:
- Estes Park Chamber of Commerce, 500 Big Thompson Avenue, Estes Park, CO 80517, (970) 586-4431 or 1-800-44-ESTES
- Grand Lake Chamber of Commerce, P.O. Box 57, Grand Lake, CO 80477, (970) 627-3402, 1-800-531-1019.

A NOTE ABOUT SAFETY

Safety is an important concern in all outdoor activities. No guidebook can alert you to every hazard or anticipate the limitations of every reader. Therefore, the descriptions of roads, trails, routes, and natural features in this book are not representations that a particular place or excursion will be safe for your party. When you follow any of the routes described in this book, you assume responsibility for your own safety. Under normal conditions, such excursions require the usual attention to traffic, road and trail conditions, weather, terrain, the capabilities of your party, and other factors. Keeping informed on current conditions and exercising common sense are the keys to a safe, enjoyable outing.

—The Mountaineers

CHAPTER

2

East Side Hikes

The east side of Rocky Mountain National Park is its busiest. It is home to the park headquarters and visitor center, Glacier Basin and Moraine Park Campgrounds (the park's largest), and the extremely popular Bear Lake, Glacier Gorge, and Cub Lake trailheads. The region offers hikes of every length and difficulty, delivering some of the park's most dramatic scenery on some of its shortest trails. The east side is also an easy drive from Denver and neighboring cities. As a result, the east side draws many more visitors than the west. Consequently, to enjoy a measure of solitude amid this spectacular beauty, choose trails with low or moderate levels of use, hike early in the morning, and avoid weekends. Alternatively, arrive after Labor Day, when visitation drops dramatically.

Avoid parking hassles by using the park's free shuttle bus. During the summer, lots at the Bear Lake and Glacier Gorge trailheads are usually full by midmorning. The bus is a convenient way to reach both trailheads, and it allows you to begin and end your hikes at different trailheads, thereby greatly expanding your hiking options. Parking for the shuttle is located on Bear Lake Road, 5.1 miles from its junction with US Highway 36. The bus is free and in summer makes the run about every 15 minutes, from approximately 9:45 A.M. to 5:30 P.M. A shuttle bus also services Moraine Park Campground, Fern/Cub Lake Trailheads, Moraine

_.useum, Hollowell Park, and Glacier Basin Campground.
_.eck with the Park Service for a current schedule.

When choosing a hike in Moraine Park (Cub Lake and Fern Lake Trailheads), Hollowell Park (Mill Creek Basin Trailhead), Bierstadt Moraine, Glacier Gorge, or Bear Lake, consult the Bear Lake Hiking Map on page 98 for additional hiking options. The area offers many lovely one-way hikes, which are possible using two cars or the shuttle bus. By beginning at Bear Lake, large elevation gains can sometimes be avoided.

In addition, young families should note that several east-side hikes are accessible to strollers and wheelchairs. Stroller-accessible trails include Moraine Park (Hike 3), portions of the Bear Lake Trail (Hike 11), and the Alluvial Fan Trail (Hike 22). Wheelchair users can access three very lovely trails, the Beaver Boardwalk (Hike 23), Sprague Lake Trail (Hike 5), and Lily Lake Trail (Hike 26), all accessible according to uniform federal accessibility standards.

1

Arch Rocks and the Pool

DIFFICULTY: easy
DISTANCE: 1.5 miles one way to Arch Rocks, 1.7 miles one
    way to the Pool
USAGE: high
STARTING ELEVATION: 8,155 feet; elevation gain, 45 feet
    to Arch Rocks, 245 feet to the Pool
BACKCOUNTRY CAMPSITE: 1.2 miles from the trailhead
SEASON: spring, summer, fall
MAP: USGS 7.5-minute McHenrys Peak

The trail to the Pool is a fine hike, especially for children. It offers a level trail, great diversity of vegetation, climbable boulders, access to a clear river, fishing, and good picnic spots. In the early

Arch Rocks

morning or at dusk, watch for deer in Moraine Park and near the trailhead. To avoid crowds on this popular trail, hike early or late in the day. Bring plenty of drinks; this hike can be hot and dry in summer.

Drive US Highway 36 to Bear Lake Road, located 0.2 mile west of Beaver Meadows Entrance Station and 2.7 miles from Deer Ridge Junction. Drive Bear Lake Road 1.2 miles to the first road on the right, which heads toward Moraine Park Campground. Take this road and drive 0.5 mile; turn left just before the campground entrance and follow signs for the Cub and Fern Lake Trailheads. Drive 0.7 mile to the Cub Lake Trailhead and then go 1 mile to the parking lot for the Fern Lake Trailhead.

The wide, smooth, sandy trail begins at the west end of the parking lot and parallels the Big Thompson River on the left. Bordering the trail are bracken ferns, Rocky Mountain maples, and aspens. By the river, narrowleaf cottonwood, water birch, and thinleaf alder shade the banks. All contribute gay reds and yellows to the fall landscape, making this trail an excellent autumn hike.

Small pebbly beaches invite exploration of the riverbank. This area is prime beaver habitat. Notice the conical stumps of aspens cut by beaver. A beaver can fell a 3-inch-diameter tree in less than 10 minutes. Beavers make good use of the aspen, eating its bark and using its branches to build their dams. Look carefully along the river for evidence of beaver activity.

Large boulders are common here. Some were deposited by the glacier that retreated from this valley 13,000 to 15,000 years ago. Other boulders—the more angular ones—are probably of more recent origin, having fallen from the high cliffs nearby. Youngsters will enjoy the safe climbing provided by the boulders. They can also search for ghoulish faces and creatures in the pattern of cracks and crevices on the rocks.

After 1.2 miles on this nearly level trail, come to Arch Rocks Campsite, an excellent backcountry destination for beginning campers. Around dusk look for beavers, which are primarily nocturnal, to emerge from their lodges and begin their work.

The stretch of trail between Arch Rocks Campsite and Arch Rocks (0.3 mile farther) offers a series of lovely, easily accessible picnic spots by the river. Anglers will want to try their luck trout fishing in the swiftly flowing water. Numerous flowers and large rocks enhance the scene.

At 1.5 miles from the trailhead, arrive at Arch Rocks, where several huge boulders form an arch over the trail. For the best view of the rocks, walk under them and turn around. Arch Rocks is a good turnaround point for hikers who wish to avoid uphill walking.

Just 0.2 mile beyond Arch Rocks is the Pool. As the Big Thompson River flows between steep rock walls, the water's motion has eroded a pool, whose calm contrasts with torrents crashing over rocks as the river rounds a bend. The sun-drenched flat rocks by the Pool are popular for picnicking. The substantial bridge over the Pool is also a good place to observe the powerful flow of the water.

Watch at the Pool for the curious dipper, or water ouzel. This brown bird, resembling a large wren, acrobatically flies in and out of the rushing water looking for small fish and aquatic insects. The dipper is able to walk on the bottom of streams, swim underwater, and fly behind waterfalls. Watch them disappear again and again in the rushing water. The dipper builds its nest on rocky ledges, often within the spray of a waterfall, where its eggs are safe from predators.

HIKING OPTIONS:

(1) At the Pool, the trail is joined by the path from Cub Lake, which lies 1 mile to the southeast. For a wonderful loop hike of 6 miles, start at the Cub Lake Trailhead, hike to Cub Lake, and then continue to the Pool and return along the Fern Lake Trail. This loop is delightful from either direction, but beginning at the Cub Lake Trailhead it affords fine views of the Front Range as you head west (see Hike 2). (2) Fern Falls is 1 mile west of the Pool on the Fern Lake Trail. The shady, steep trail switchbacks through thick subalpine forest and gains 480 feet elevation. The falls are perhaps unspectacular for the effort required. (3) Fern Lake is 2.1 miles from the Pool on the Fern Lake Trail and requires an additional 730-foot elevation gain from Fern Falls. The trail is strenuous. From the Fern Lake Trailhead, Fern Lake is 3.8 miles one way, with an elevation gain of 1,375 feet.

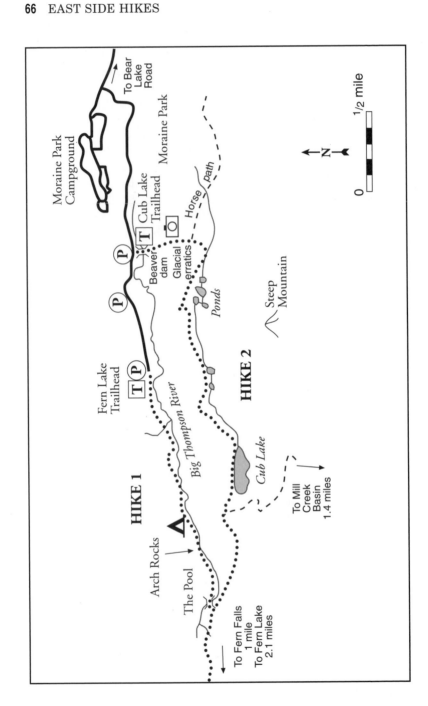

2

Cub Lake and the Pool Loop

DIFFICULTY: moderate
DISTANCE: 2.3 miles one way to Cub Lake; 6-mile loop via
    the Pool
USAGE: high
STARTING ELEVATION: 8,080 feet; elevation gain, 540 feet
BACKCOUNTRY CAMPSITE: 3.8 miles from trailhead
SEASON: spring, summer, fall
MAPS: USGS 7.5-minute Longs Peak, McHenrys Peak

This hike is a jewel. Few trails in the park offer such diversity. The trail sparkles with wildflowers of innumerable variety. It is rich with birds and wildlife. Beautiful and interesting sights and sounds appear at every bend, including beaver dams, rushing streams, lily-filled ponds, and climbable boulders of all shapes and sizes. For bird watchers, wildlife enthusiasts, and flower lovers, this trail is a favorite. Hike in the early morning or late afternoon to avoid the midday crowds.

Drive to the Cub Lake Trailhead, as described in Hike 1. The trailhead is at the west end of the parking lot. If the lot is full, drive 0.3 mile farther to an additional parking area. From mid-June to mid-August, hikers may also use the park shuttle bus.

The trail begins by crossing a bridge over a branch of the Big Thompson River. The bridge provides a good view of a large beaver dam. Look for signs of recent beaver activity. Return at dusk for a chance to see these nocturnal rodents at work. In the fall, when beavers must gather food for the long winter to come, they may be out during the day. A family of nine beavers may consume a ton of bark over the winter.

Shortly after the first bridge, cross a second bridge. This is a good place for an early detour to explore the streamside environment. Willow and river birch are plentiful, as are numerous wildflowers, including yellow shrubby cinquefoil, blue chimingbells, and pink and violet shooting stars.

A maze of paths made by deer and fishermen leads along the river's edge, where pebbly beaches, cruising ducks, or trout anglers may interest your youngsters. The area between the bridges and along the river is also an excellent place to look for deer. Elk appear here in the fall.

For a closer look at the work of beavers, take the first path on the right, about 10 feet after the second bridge. There you find trees cut by beaver, evidenced by conical stumps and teeth marks.

For a beautiful flower-filled meadow with a backdrop of the majestic Front Range, take the second spur trail on the right after the bridge. Please be careful not to trample or pick the flowers.

Return to the main trail. From the second bridge, the main trail rolls gently through montane meadowlands. Even the youngest feet can negotiate this smooth trail. Early morning hikers find many types of animal tracks in the soft dirt. In summer look for the tracks of deer, marmots, rabbits, ground squirrels, and chipmunks. Elk tracks appear in the spring and fall.

The trail follows the western edge of Moraine Park. Lookouts to the east are tremendous places to watch for deer at sunset. To the right are a wealth of climbable rocks. Small mammals are plentiful here, including chipmunks and golden-mantled ground squirrels. Watch also for marmots, which are particularly easy to spot on sunny days, when they enjoy napping on the sun-warmed rocks.

The trail weaves through mature ponderosa pines, a conifer with reddish, deeply furrowed bark, needles 5 to 8 inches long, and bark that smells like vanilla (truly!). Ponderosa pines are a favorite of the porcupine, which you may see napping on a limb. Never disturb one of these prickly rodents, each of which carries more than 30,000 quills.

On the left, groves of aspens add brilliant color to the trail in the fall. One mature grove is home to a wide variety of cavity-dwelling birds. When aspens age and soften, they are often full of insects, which provide abundant food for birds such as woodpeckers, nuthatches, and chickadees. Listen for the tap-tap of the woodpecker. Once a hole is made, the bird probes for insects with its long tongue.

At 0.4 mile a horse path joins the trail from the east. Continue south on the main trail, which shortly turns west to follow a slow-moving stream. This portion of the hike is particularly fun for observant and imaginative children, who can see fantastic things in the giant, oddly shaped rocks—a whale with its snout on the

Colorado blue columbine, the state flower

trail, a leering dwarf with a pointed ear, and a giant dinosaur egg. On the left are abandoned beaver ponds, where leopard frogs, whirligig beetles, iridescent blue dragonflies, and water boatmen now thrive.

At 1.8 miles the trail begins to switchback to Cub Lake, becoming more rocky and shady in a mixed forest of conifers and aspens. After a relatively steep ascent (during which you may startle a deer in its daytime forest retreat), the trail levels out not far from the lake.

Cub Lake is wonderful. In summer, it is covered with yellow pond lilies. Its shady banks make a perfect picnic spot. Ducks on the banks join you, as will numerous small mammals. To the west, 12,922-foot Stones Peak rises majestically above the lake.

To hike the 6-mile loop by way of the Pool and Fern Lake Trail, continue on the trail along Cub Lake's north shore. At the west end of the lake, the trail enters lodgepole pines and in 0.2 mile meets the trail from Mill Creek Basin entering from the south. Keep right in a westerly direction, descending slightly along a partially exposed north-facing slope with very good views. Reach the Pool 1 mile from Cub Lake. To complete the loop, turn right on the Fern Lake Trail and descend slightly for 1.7 miles to the trailhead (see Hike 1). From the Fern Lake Trailhead, walk or ride 1 mile down the road (east) to the Cub Lake Trailhead.

HIKING OPTIONS:

(1) Combine the hike to Cub Lake with the hike from Hollowell Park to Mill Creek Basin for a one-way 5.4-mile trip (elevation gain 600 feet). A second car or shuttle bus ride would be needed. See Hike 4 for a detailed description of the hike to Mill Creek Basin. (2) Hike mostly downhill from Bear Lake, via Bierstadt Lake and Mill Creek Basin, to Cub Lake and from there to the Cub Lake Trailhead, for a total distance of 6.5 miles. Again, the shuttle bus or a second car would be needed. See the Bear Lake Hiking Map on page 98.

3

Moraine Park

DIFFICULTY: nature stroll, handicapped access with
    assistance
DISTANCE: 0.25 mile one way
USAGE: moderate
STARTING ELEVATION: 8,000 feet; elevation gain, none
BACKCOUNTRY CAMPSITE: none
SEASON: spring, summer, fall
MAP: USGS 7.5-minute Longs Peak

This hike is a fine walk in a large, lovely meadow, brimming with wildflowers and dramatic sights of the glacial forces that formed Moraine Park thousands of years ago.

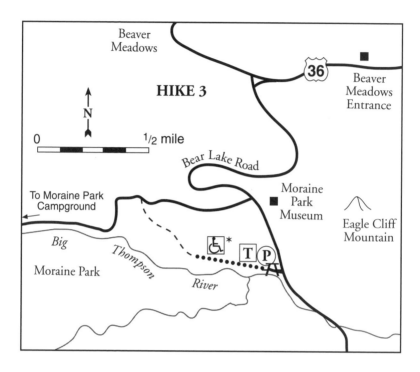

Drive to Bear Lake Road, as described in Hike 1. Turn left on Bear Lake Road and drive 1.6 miles to a parking area on the right, at the eastern end of Moraine Park. The parking area is 0.4 mile south of the Moraine Park Museum. The trail begins at the west end of the parking lot.

This hike at the eastern edge of Moraine Park starts on a paved road closed to traffic. The road begins at the picnic area near the parking lot and travels into Moraine Park along the Big Thompson River. To the west are excellent views of the Front Range. At dawn and dusk, willows by the river may hide feeding deer in the summer and elk in the colorful fall. In spring and summer, wildflowers are abundant in the meadow. After a short distance, the pavement ends, replaced by a wide, level path that is still accessible to wheelchairs and strollers. After 0.25 mile, the trail narrows. Visitors in wheelchairs must turn back. Hikers may proceed on the narrow path for another 0.5 mile to explore the meadow. This trail eventually leads to Upper Beaver Meadows, an uphill hike of approximately 1.75 miles. This portion of the trail is not recommended because of its heavy use by horseback riders and its proximity to US Highway 36. To return to the trailhead, turn around and retrace your steps.

The mammoth glacier that sculpted this area left its mark everywhere. The large boulders in the meadow are glacial erratics, which were torn from the mountains by the moving ice, which carried them downslope to be dropped far from where they originated. To the left is the glacier's south lateral moraine. This long pile of rock debris, now thickly forested, was gathered, pushed, and finally deposited here by the rivers of ice that flowed from Forest Canyon, Spruce Canyon, and Odessa Gorge. These ice streams united to form one massive glacier, whose depth as it entered Moraine Park ranged from 750 to 1,500 feet.

More information on the history, geology, flora, and fauna of Moraine Park can be found in the booklet "Moraine Park Museum and Interpretive Trail," published by the Rocky Mountain Nature Association and available at most park visitor centers. Visitors interested in geology should visit the recently renovated Moraine Park Museum, which offers ingenious interactive exhibits illustrating the geologic history of the park.

4

Mill Creek Basin

DIFFICULTY: easy
DISTANCE: 1.6 miles one way
USAGE: moderate
STARTING ELEVATION: 8,339 feet; elevation gain,
     600 feet
BACKCOUNTRY CAMPSITE: 1.6 and 1.8 miles from
     trailhead
SEASON: spring, summer, fall
MAPS: USGS 7.5-minute Longs Peak, McHenrys Peak

Beginning in a dry meadow with expansive views and bordered by forested moraines, this easy hike offers big sky, sagebrush, and wildflowers on a dusty trail. A clear running stream with a beaver lodge adds interest to the latter part of the trail. Although this

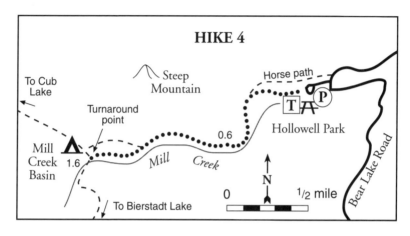

hike does not dazzle with dramatic scenery, it is uncrowded and excellent for spotting red-tailed hawks or hiking under the stars. The dusty trail has a typically Western feel, ideal for parents who can spin a tale or two about the Old West.

Drive to Bear Lake Road, as described in Hike 1. Follow the road 3.6 miles, and then turn right at Hollowell Park onto an unpaved road and continue to the parking area for the Mill Creek Basin Trailhead at the end of the road.

Head due west from the trailhead on the clearly marked trail through a large open meadow. The first 0.6 mile of sandy trail is smooth and level. Even your toddler can make good time along this section. Far to the south, Longs Peak, the highest peak in Rocky Mountain National Park, rises to 14,255 feet.

The trail is fragrant with the scent of sagebrush, which covers the meadow in silvery green. Naturalists believe that the muted greens of dry meadow plants protect them from the intense heat and ultraviolet light of the sun. Look to the moister, shadier areas near Mill Creek to see darker, lusher greens.

The first half mile of this hike is filled with the sights, sounds, and smells of the Old West. Your "Wild West" tales will be effectively punctuated by the thundering of horses' hooves, for this trail is popular with the horse concessions. Mix in the facts below for an authentic Rocky Mountain tale.

Two hundred years ago, two Native American tribes, the Utes and Arapahos, used this area for seasonal hunting and foraging and fought frequently (perhaps on this site) to maintain their shares of the territory. Indian women probably gathered the plants of this meadow for medicine and food. Because plants comprised 80 percent of the Indians' total food supply, women were the backbone of their society. Notice, for example, the red Indian paintbrush beside the trail. The flower looks like a ragged brush dipped in red-orange paint. The Indians ate this flower and used its roots to make medicine to thin the blood, cure nervous disorders, and prevent fainting.

The trail heads south to meet Mill Creek, passing aspens that have been grazed by wintering herds of elk. When food is scarce, as it is each winter, the elk eat the inner bark of the aspen, leaving black scars on the yellowish bark. Although you will probably not see elk here in summer, notice how the twisted branches of the sagebrush look like fallen antlers, and how the dry, weathered wood by the path resembles bleached bones.

Examining (not picking!) wildflowers in Hollowell Park

The meeting of the trail with Mill Creek at 0.6 mile makes a very pleasant rest stop. The coolness of the fast-flowing creek and the shade of the trees are welcome relief from the sunny, dry meadow. This spot may be a good final destination for your youngest hikers, for there is a lot to explore at the creek.

A little scouting nearby reveals a beaver dam and lodge. Farther up the trail aspens have been cut by beavers for use in constructing their dams and lodges.

White trappers came here for beaver in the 1800s, after eastern trappers had decimated the beaver population east of the Mississippi. Beaver were in great demand in the early nineteenth century for men's hats. The beaver hat was so popular in those days that the word *beaver* was used as slang for *hat*. Fortunately for the western beaver, fashion changed in the late 1800s, when the use of silk in top hats spelled salvation for the large rodent.

The trail continues west along Mill Creek, rising gradually to Mill Creek Basin, 1.6 miles from the trailhead. Tall purple chimingbells appear, which, true to their name, resemble long stalks of bells. Look also for bedstraw, another tall plant with numerous small four-petaled white flowers. Early settlers used the stalks of bedstraw as mattress stuffing and its seeds as a coffee substitute.

Mill Creek Basin is a pretty meadow that lies between Mount Wuh (10,761 feet) to the west and Steep Mountain (9,538 feet) to the northeast. A campsite at the basin provides a fine backpacking destination. From this point, trails lead north to Cub Lake and south to Bierstadt Lake. More scenic trails to these destinations are described in Hikes 2 and 16.

Return to the trailhead by retracing your steps. Walking back through Hollowell Park, notice the difference in the south- and north-facing slopes that flank the meadow. Large ponderosa pine, which require sunny, dry conditions, are widely spaced along the south-facing slopes, while dense, dark green forests of Douglas firs, which prefer a cooler, moister environment, cover the mountainsides facing north. This pattern of growth occurs throughout the park. In fact, when Enos Mills, the "father" of Rocky Mountain National Park, was afflicted with temporary snow blindness, he determined his direction by using the type of tree growth as an indicator.

HIKING OPTIONS:

Using the park shuttle bus, hike a very scenic and varied trail from Bear Lake to Bierstadt Lake, and from there to Mill Creek Basin and Hollowell Park, for a total distance of 4.3 miles. See the map on page 98.

5

Sprague Lake

DIFFICULTY: nature stroll, handicapped access according to uniform federal accessibility standards
DISTANCE: 0.5 mile around lake
USAGE: high
STARTING ELEVATION: 8,710 feet; elevation gain, none
BACKCOUNTRY CAMPSITE: Handicamp 0.3 miles from trailhead
SEASON: spring, summer, fall
MAP: USGS 7.5-minute Longs Peak

This very easy, half-mile loop trail is a wonderful introduction to hiking for the park's youngest visitors. The trail offers children numerous natural attractions while providing parents with a level stroll, terrific views, abundant benches, and child-tested picnic spots. This beautiful trail is absolutely perfect for wheelchairs and strollers. Anglers in the family will enjoy trying for elusive cutthroat trout; children will rejoice in the many mallard ducklings.

Drive to Bear Lake Road, as described in Hike 1. Follow Bear Lake Road 5.7 miles to the well-marked turn for Sprague Lake. Turn left and drive to the parking lot at the end of the road. The lake is to the left of the parking area.

Begin the hike at the lake's edge and walk clockwise. Before you set out, be sure to purchase a guide to the Sprague Lake Nature Trail from the dispenser at the start of the trail ($1). The 14-page illustrated booklet provides information on the history, flora, and fauna of the lake and contains a useful schematic drawing of the peaks visible from the east side of the lake. The booklet is also available at park visitor centers.

The stroll around the lake offers many opportunities for youngsters to view birds, insects, and small mammals. The air is rich with chirping, quacking, and chattering. Children can enjoy watching mallards paddling with their ducklings in tow. Chipmunks and golden-mantled ground squirrels are also abundant near the lake. At the southwest end of the lake is a deserted beaver lodge, and you may spot a trespassing muskrat, if you're lucky.

Also fascinating to the youngsters is the thriving insect life. Diving beetles, water scavengers, whirligig beetles, caddisflies, dragonflies, water boatmen, and midges appear by the thousands. It would be wise to bring along insect repellent for mosquitos and fun to tote a small jar for bug hunting. (Be sure to free all insects unharmed after observing them.) Less obvious but also present are leopard frogs, chorus frogs, and western toads.

Numerous benches along the shore provide majestic views of the lake and surrounding mountains. Also located at intervals around the lake are small wooden platforms with railings. Built over the water, these platforms allow children to observe the water safely without the danger of a steep fall.

Sprague Lake, like all lakes in the park, is too cold for swimming. Except in the lake's shallowest places, the water rarely exceeds 60 degrees Fahrenheit. Fishing is possible here, as early settlers of the area stocked the lake with trout. The chance of catching one is slim, but this does not discourage the ever-present anglers in their small boats or hip boots.

The best picnic spot is exactly halfway around the lake. It offers benches and large rocks where parents can rest and set out lunch while the children play. A pebbly beach adds to the fun. The spot boasts a superb view of many high peaks. The best views are those of Hallett Peak (12,713 feet) and adjacent Flattop Mountain (12,324 feet).

On the east side of the lake, a spur trail heading left leads to Handicamp, a backcountry campsite for wheelchair campers. It is a lovely spot among quaking aspens, only a short hike down a level trail. For more information on Handicamp, inquire at the visitor center at Park Headquarters.

Continuing clockwise around the lake, the trail enters the shade of lodgepole pines. The trail eventually emerges via bridges and boardwalks at the northwest edge of the lake, where the trail began.

Hikers resting beneath Hallet Peak at Sprague Lake

HIKING OPTIONS:

For an additional short hike in this area, find the Glacier Creek Trailhead on the southeast side of the Sprague Lake parking lot. A short walk of 0.6 mile along sparkling Glacier Creek is a pleasant and effortless stroll. The scenic banks of the creek invite exploration and offer quiet places for lovely picnics. Children will love to dip their toes in the icy water. Aspen and willow provide high color in autumn.

6

Boulder Brook/Alberta Falls Loop

DIFFICULTY: strenuous
DISTANCE: 5.6 miles one way
USAGE: mostly low, high at end
STARTING ELEVATION: 8,840 feet; elevation gain,
    1,450 feet
BACKCOUNTRY CAMPSITE: 1.9 miles from the trailhead
SEASON: summer, fall
MAPS: USGS 7.5-minute Longs Peak, McHenrys Peak

This fine, demanding hike is enjoyable in any season but is especially magnificent in the fall. The trail leads steeply up a
mountainside covered with aspens, then levels out amid panoramic views of Glacier Gorge and the Bear Lake area. The last
part of the hike takes you down through Glacier Gorge and by
the popular and beautiful Alberta Falls.

    Drive to Bear Lake Road, as described in Hike 1. Turn left and
follow Bear Lake Road 6.5 miles to a parking area on the right
side of the road. The trailhead, marked Storm Pass, is across the
road, just 0.1 mile east of the well-marked Bierstadt Lake
Trailhead on the north side of the road, where there is also parking. If all the roadside parking places are full, backtrack 1.4 miles
on Bear Lake Road and park in the shuttle bus parking area. The
shuttle bus will bring you to the trailhead. Note that this hike
ends at the Glacier Gorge Trailhead, 2 miles farther west on Bear
Lake Road. Use the Bear Lake shuttle bus to return to your car.
If a longer hike or complete loop is desired, see the hiking options
described below.

    The trail begins at a large sign for the Storm Pass Trailhead.
Follow the trail indicated by the sign, heading east along the
willow-lined bank of Glacier Creek. To the west, Hallett Peak,
Flattop Mountain, and Chiefs Head Peak rise dramatically above
the creek.

    Shortly cross a bridge over the creek and head into a forest
of lodgepole pines. When the trail forks, stay to the right, on the
main trail. Continue to a junction with trails to Bear Lake (right)

and Wind River and Storm Pass (left). Continue straight ahead as indicated by the sign for the Boulder Brook Trail.

Boulder Brook runs parallel to the trail. The brook's banks are carpeted with pine needles and shaded by aspens and pines. Unfortunately, many aspens have been scarred by vandals. Please discourage this practice, for if cuts girdle the tree, the aspen may die.

Aspens are a valuable food source for many of the park's animals. Deer, elk, and moose browse the aspen's twigs, bark, and foliage; beavers and rabbits eat its bark, foliage, and buds; and the hardy ptarmigan feeds on its winter buds.

Boulder Brook offers many pleasant spots where hikers can sit on large rocks, watch the cascading water, and listen to the musical brook. The ground cover by the brook is wild blueberry, and in late summer it provides a delicious snack. As the trail continues to climb, small cascading waterfalls appear. Gray rocks, white rapids, streamside flowers, and flickering aspen leaves create a lovely scene.

At 0.7 mile from the trailhead, cross the brook. After two more crossings, the trail becomes less steep and more open. Wind, rocks, and the sounds of water predominate. A forest fire in 1900 cleared this area of trees, and new growth has come slowly. Enjoy good views of the Mummy Range to the north, Hallett Peak and Flattop Mountain to the west, and Half Mountain close by to the northwest.

A fourth crossing of the stream at 1.9 miles brings you to two backcountry campsites, Boulder Brook #1 and #2. Continue past the campsites to the junction with the North Longs Peak Trail, 2.3 miles from the trailhead. Turn right and follow the North Longs Peak Trail toward Glacier Gorge Junction.

The trail is now considerably easier. Relax and enjoy the superlative views, again made possible by the forest fire. Walk west along the north-facing slope for 2.2 miles (the Park Service sign indicates 3 miles). Happily, the trail heads downhill for most of the remaining distance. Dramatically shaped limber pines line the path, framing views of the surrounding mountains. Andrews Glacier can be seen clearly ahead, hanging majestically between Otis and Taylor Peaks.

Larger boulders and more aspens appear as the trail nears Glacier Gorge. Rock-strewn Half Mountain is on the left. After 2.1 miles on the North Longs Peak Trail (4.4 miles from the

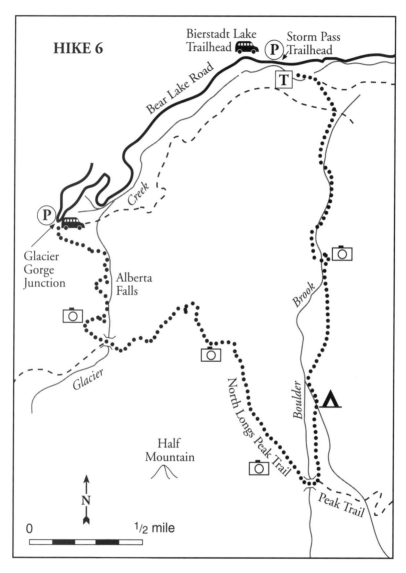

HIKE 6

Bierstadt Lake Trailhead

Storm Pass Trailhead

Bear Lake Road

Creek

Glacier Gorge Junction

Alberta Falls

Glacier

Brook

Boulder

North Longs Peak Trail

Half Mountain

Peak Trail

N

0   1/2 mile

trailhead), come to a substantial bridge over Glacier Creek. The orange rock walls rise steeply to create a deep narrow canyon. In autumn the aspens in this area are stunning. After the bridge, the trail heads uphill a short distance to the junction with the Glacier Gorge Trail. Take the trail that heads downhill to the north, toward Glacier Gorge Junction and Alberta Falls.

The dry rocky trail to Alberta Falls switchbacks down the mountainside. On these rocky slopes look for marmots and pikas. Before you reach the falls, there are good overlooks into the gorge to the right. Listen for the falls below.

At 5 miles from the trailhead, arrive at Alberta Falls. Only 0.6 mile of easy downhill trail remains. (For a detailed description of this portion of the trail, see Hike 7.) At Glacier Gorge Junction, take the shuttle bus back to your car.

HIKING OPTIONS:

As an alternative to the shuttle bus, a 2.3-mile trail parallels Bear Lake Road, leading back to the Boulder Brook Trail. The total round-trip distance with this extension is 8.1 miles. Pick up this trail at Glacier Gorge Junction. Upon reaching the Boulder Brook Trail, turn left to return to the trailhead.

7

Alberta Falls

DIFFICULTY: easy
DISTANCE: 0.6 mile one way
USAGE: high
STARTING ELEVATION: 9,240 feet; elevation gain,
       160 feet
BACKCOUNTRY CAMPSITE: none
SEASON: summer, fall
MAP: USGS 7.5-minute McHenrys Peak

This short but rewarding hike leads to one of the park's most impressive waterfalls. Because the waterfall is also among the most accessible, this trail is extremely popular. To avoid the crowds, hike very early or late in the day, or reserve this hike for autumn, when the foliage is spectacular and the traffic is lighter.

Drive to Bear Lake Road, as described in Hike 1. Follow Bear Lake Road 8.5 miles to the parking area for Glacier Gorge Junction. The trailhead is across the road from the south side of the lot. Because parking is very limited at Glacier Gorge Junction, the free park shuttle bus is highly recommended. Parking for the shuttle bus is on Bear Lake Road 5.1 miles from its junction with US Highway 36. The bus runs about every 15 minutes in the summer. Check at a park visitor center for details.

For the first quarter mile, the trail to Alberta Falls is wide, smooth, and fairly level. In this quarter mile, you cross four wooden bridges over Glacier Creek. These bridges provide interest from the start for the youngest hikers. The trail follows the creek through stands of aspen, fir, and spruce. Note that many aspens have been scarred by vandals. Sadly, this phenomenon is common along the more popular trails in the park. Carving not only permanently disfigures the trees but can be detrimental to their health. Please point this out to your youngsters and heartily discourage it.

Alberta Falls

The wealth of aspens on this trail makes it an excellent hike in the fall, when the leaves turn brilliant shades of yellow-gold and provide a stunning contrast to the dark green of the conifers and the deep blue of the western sky.

After a quarter mile, the trail quickly becomes steeper and rockier. Wild blueberry covers the ground along the trail. This stretch is hot in summer because the young trees that line the path provide little shade. The mountainside was burned by a forest fire in 1900 and has not fully recovered. Consequently, hikers have fine views of the Glacier Gorge area and surrounding peaks. To the north, look for the distinctive peaks of the Mummy Range, including Mount Chapin (12,454 feet), Mount Chiquita (13,069 feet), and Ypsilon Mountain (13,514 feet), with its permanent snowfield in the shape of a Y. To the west, Flattop Mountain (12,324 feet) and the dramatic angular profile of Hallett Peak (12,713 feet) are visible.

Over much of this short trail, hikers hear the rushing water of Glacier Creek as it crashes through Alberta Falls. The sound of the falls teases, growing louder with each bend in the trail, then fading with each switchback. The sound entices you to travel a little faster up the last steep sections of the trail.

Alberta Falls is truly impressive. The falls and narrow gorge reveal dramatically the power of running water to sculpt and erode. Welcome spray cools and refreshes after the warm ascent. For an even better view of Alberta Falls, climb (with supervision of children and *extreme* caution) on the rocks above the trail toward the head of the falls. There, the power of the water rushing over the rocks is felt and heard with a thrilling intensity.

HIKING OPTIONS:

(1) Continue 1.9 miles and climb 540 feet to Mills Lake (see Hike 8). (2) Continue 2.1 miles and climb 780 feet to the Loch (see Hike 9). (3) Continue 2.5 miles and climb 820 feet to Lake Haiyaha (see Hike 15). (4) From the Glacier Gorge Trailhead, Bear Lake is only 0.5 mile by a clearly marked trail, which heads northwest. For information on Bear Lake Hikes, see the Bear Lake Hiking Map on page 98.

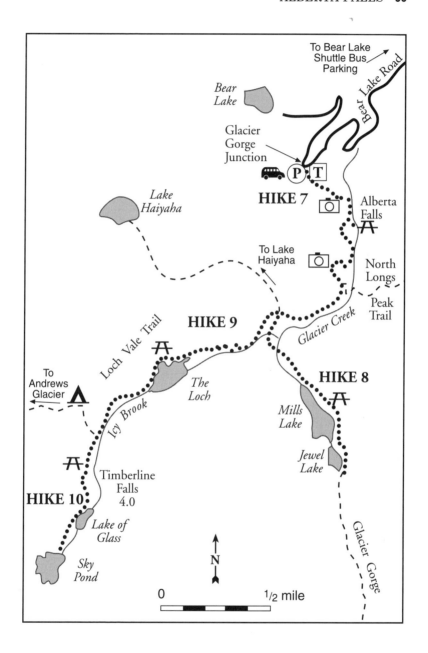

To Bear Lake
Shuttle Bus
Parking

Bear Lake Road

Bear
Lake

Glacier
Gorge
Junction

P T

HIKE 7

Lake
Haiyaha

Alberta
Falls

To Lake
Haiyaha

North
Longs

Peak
Trail

Glacier Creek

Loch Vale Trail

HIKE 9

To
Andrews
Glacier

The
Loch

HIKE 8

Mills
Lake

Icy Brook

Jewel
Lake

Timberline
Falls
4.0

HIKE 10

Lake of
Glass

Sky
Pond

N

Glacier Gorge

0   1/2 mile

8

Mills Lake

DIFFICULTY: moderate
DISTANCE: 2.5 miles one way
USAGE: high
STARTING ELEVATION: 9,240 feet; elevation gain,
        700 feet
BACKCOUNTRY CAMPSITE: 3.5 miles from the trailhead
SEASON: summer, fall
MAP: USGS 7.5-minute McHenrys Peak

The moderately challenging hike to Mills Lake is extremely scenic. The trail offers sweeping alpine views and verdant subalpine forest with fine wildflowers. Upon reaching the lake, you are rewarded with one of the most beautiful cirques in the park. The lake's dramatic reflections are unequaled. Early morning is the best time to arrive, before wind ripples the lake's surface and hikers crowd its shores. Because the first portion of the trail climbs an open, sunny slope, bring sun protection and plenty of water.

Hike to Alberta Falls, as described in Hike 7. Above the falls, the trail continues to climb the rocky slope amid fine views to the north of the Mummy Range, Mount Chapin (12,454 feet), Mount Chiquita (13,069 feet), and Ypsilon Mountain (13,514 feet); to the west are Flattop Mountain (12,324 feet) and the precipitous Hallett Peak (12,713 feet).

The trail follows Glacier Creek. For good views of the rushing water, carefully approach the edge and peer into the gorge just before the trail heads sharply west, away from the creek. In these rocky environs, watch for quick-moving pikas and indolent marmots.

Shortly, the North Longs Peak Trail enters from the left (east). Keep right on the Glacier Gorge Trail, following the signs for Loch Vale and Mills Lake. A welcome stretch of trail descends into a pretty subalpine forest. Notice the conical aspen stumps with teeth marks—sure signs of beavers at work.

Reflection in Mills Lake

At 1.9 miles arrive at a junction with the trails to Loch Vale (Hike 9) and to Lake Haiyaha (Hike 15). Take the trail to the left, which leads to Glacier Gorge. The sign indicates Mills Lake and Black Lake.

A short, shady walk leads to the crossing of a charming stream named Icy Brook. The trail then briefly enters denser woods, passing an area littered with glacial erratics, large boulders dropped by the glacier that flowed through this gorge. Soon the trail completely disappears on bedrock, but the way is clearly marked by rock cairns.

Limber pines grow seemingly straight out of bedrock. These hardy conifers thrive at timberline and on rocky ledges, where most other trees are unable to survive. Limber pines are magnificent both in life and in death. The sculptural, twisting shapes of long-dead limber pines give this rugged landscape an eerie beauty.

The trail briefly leaves the bedrock to cross Glacier Creek amid a variety of wildflowers. After another short segment over rock, the trail arrives at Mills Lake, 2.5 miles from the trailhead. Lying in a deep basin scooped out by a massive glacier, the lake is truly magnificent. Its rocky shore invites you to sit and appreciate the deep beauty of the place. In summer, vivid pink elephanthead flowers brighten the scene.

Arrive in the morning, when the lake is still, to enjoy its incomparable reflections of Longs Peak, Pagoda Peak, and the Keyboard of the Winds. The name Keyboard of the Winds derives from the strange organlike sounds that a rare wind makes as it blows across the rock spires. Even if you've missed this singular concert, there is always music at Mills Lake. The quiet sounds of the lake, the wind, and the birds overhead play their own delicate melodies. Mills Lake makes a superb picnic spot. In autumn, look for wild blueberries near the shore.

This special lake was named for Enos Mills (1870–1922), who was instrumental in creating Rocky Mountain National Park. Mills was a self-educated naturalist, avid mountaineer (he climbed Longs Peak over 250 times), and pioneer in the conservation movement. He dedicated years of his life to create Rocky Mountain National Park. It is fitting that such an outstanding lake bear his name. Mills wrote: "A climb up the Rockies will develop a love for nature, strengthen one's appreciation of the beautiful world outdoors, and put one in tune with the Infinite. The Rockies are . . . singularly rich in mountain scenes which stir one's blood and which strengthen and sweeten life." Hikers to his lake will agree.

HIKING OPTIONS:

(1) Hike to Jewel Lake, less than 0.5 mile from the north end of Mills Lake on a trail that gains only 20 feet in elevation. To reach the small, marshy lake, continue on the trail along the eastern shore of Mills Lake. (2) Backpackers can find a fine campsite just 1 mile farther up the trail from Mills Lake. For details and a permit, contact the backcountry office at Park Headquarters. (3) The park shuttle bus enables a variety of loop hikes between Bear Lake and Glacier Gorge Junction. One excellent loop starts at Bear Lake, includes Lake Haiyaha and Mills Lake, and ends at Glacier Gorge Junction, for a total distance of 6.4 miles. See Hike 15 and the Bear Lake Hiking Map on page 98.

9

The Loch

DIFFICULTY: moderate
DISTANCE: 2.7 miles one way
USAGE: high
STARTING ELEVATION: 9,240 feet; elevation gain, 940 feet
BACKCOUNTRY CAMPSITE: 3.3 miles from the trailhead
SEASON: summer, fall
MAP: USGS 7.5-minute McHenrys Peak

This scenic trail takes you past Alberta Falls on a sunny, open slope to a beautiful mountain lake. The Loch is a fine destination, rimmed with limber pines and surrounded by distinctive peaks. The trail to the Loch is varied, offering both panoramic views and intimate forest paths. Start early to avoid the crowds on this deservedly popular hike. Be sure to bring sunscreen and an ample supply of water because the first part of the hike can be hot and sunny.

Begin this hike at Glacier Gorge Junction, as described in Hike 7. Hike the Glacier Gorge Trail past Alberta Falls to the

The Loch

Mills Lake Trail junction, as described in Hike 8. Keep straight ahead at the junction on the Loch Vale Trail.

The trail climbs gradually on an open slope with good views. After a quarter mile, as the trail swings closer to Icy Brook, aspens and yellow-flowered shrubby cinquefoil appear. The path next steeply switchbacks up a forested slope. Just before the lake are patches of snow, which last for most of the summer. Most youngsters cannot resist the novelty of throwing a few snowballs in July.

The Loch is just ahead, its rocky shore punctuated by beautiful limber pines. Limber pines are distinguished by their needles, which come in bunches of five, by their graceful, twisting contours, and by their ability to grow seemingly straight out of bedrock. The trunks of limber pines stand statuesque long after their death, resembling human torsos, their branches like arms outstretched.

High mountain walls surround the lake. To the west is the precipitous rock climber's playground known as Cathedral Wall. Taylor Glacier looms high above the Loch to the southwest. Standing at the northeastern end of the Loch, look southwest to the tiered cascade of Timberline Falls, 1.3 miles away (see Hike 10).

Ducks swim and dive in the water. The sounds of birds fill the air. Loudest is the cackle of the Clark's nutcracker, a large gray bird with handsome black and white wings. Unlike most male birds, the male Clark's nutcracker develops a brood patch, a bald area on his underside that swells with blood vessels shortly before his mate lays her eggs. The male nutcracker, who shares the duty of sitting on the eggs, uses this patch to warm them.

Anglers frequent the Loch to cast across its surface, enjoying the scenery and hoping for trout. If you plan to fish, check with the Park Service for current regulations.

The lake's rocky northern shore is an excellent place for a picnic but may be crowded. A pleasant trail leads around the lake, where many private spots can be found. The path is lovely, shady, and flower-filled. Purple mountain harebells, blue chimingbells, and purple composites attract bright green butterflies. The weathered trunks of downed trees and the sun-dappled stones combine to give the trail the feeling of a Japanese garden, where all elements are in their intended place. In such a spot, you cannot help but feel that you too are in your intended place.

HIKING OPTIONS:

(1) From the Loch, hike to Timberline Falls in 1.3 miles, Lake of Glass in 1.5 miles, and Sky Pond in 1.9 miles. Additional elevation gain for these destinations are, respectively, 270 feet, 640 feet, and 720 feet (see Hike 10). (2) Backpackers can find a campsite 0.6 mile farther up the trail from the Loch at Andrews Creek (see Hike 10). (3) If the park shuttle is operating, a variety of loop hikes are possible between Bear Lake and Glacier Gorge Junction. See the Bear Lake Hiking Map on page 98.

10

Timberline Falls, Lake of Glass, and Sky Pond

DIFFICULTY: strenuous
DISTANCE: 4 miles to Timberline Falls, 4.2 miles to Lake
      of Glass, 4.6 miles to Sky Pond—all one way
USAGE: moderate
STARTING ELEVATION: 9,240 feet; elevation gain, 1,210
      feet to Timberline Falls, 1,580 feet to Lake of Glass,
      1,660 feet to Sky Pond
BACKCOUNTRY CAMPSITE: 3.3 miles from the trailhead
SEASON: summer, fall
MAP: USGS 7.5-minute McHenrys Peak

This scenic trail leads to impressive Timberline Falls and to two starkly beautiful lakes high above Glacier Gorge. Along the way, you pass Alberta Falls and the Loch. The trail is varied and always interesting, offering both panoramic views and intimate forest settings. Reaching Lake of Glass and Sky Pond is a challenge because both lie above treeline. Nevertheless, this trail is a good one for strong young hikers, because it offers many fine intermediate destinations where you can turn back without feeling defeated. Bring sunscreen and an ample supply of water; the first portion of the hike is often hot and sunny.

Begin the hike at Glacier Gorge Junction, as described in Hike 8. Then hike to the Loch, as described in Hike 9. From the

View over Loch Vale

northeast end of the lake, look southwest to the tiered cascade of Timberline Falls, your next destination.

The trail continues around the lake's northwest side. The path is lovely, shady, and lined with flowers. After the lake, the trail runs along Icy Brook. At 0.9 mile from the eastern edge of the lake, the way splits; take the trail to the left heading toward Timberline Falls, Lake of Glass, and Sky Pond. The trail to the right leads to Andrews Glacier and backcountry campsites at Andrews Creek. Backpackers should turn right and follow the trail 0.2 mile from the junction to find the sites.

Day hikers follow the left fork. A quarter mile after the fork, arrive at the basin of Timberline Falls, an exquisite open area with the spectacular falls at its southern end. Large boulders in the basin make good perches on which to rest and watch the cascading water.

The trail leads across the basin and up alongside the waterfall. Climb with the utmost care, for the rocks are slippery. In early summer, snow or ice may make the steep climb treacherous. Depending upon conditions and the strength of your hikers, you may want to end your hike at the falls.

Above the waterfall lies a treeless, rocky landscape, for Timberline Falls was aptly named. Travel 0.2 mile over bedrock to arrive at Lake of Glass. The views to Loch Vale, and beyond to the far peaks of the north, are fabulous. The lake itself has a desolate beauty, surrounded by rocks and tundra and dark, towering peaks. To the west, massive Taylor Peak (13,153 feet) and Taylor Glacier loom high above the lake.

The easy 0.4-mile walk to Sky Pond follows the path around the lake. Sky Pond is twice as large as Lake of Glass and seems twice as desolate. The cliffs that nearly surround it are at once beautiful and menacing. Imaginative young minds may find mysterious cliff dwellings in the jagged spires or threatening faces in the rocks. The impression is that this lake is guarded. The scene has a forbidding, untamed quality. The bare, cold rocks and chilling wind at the lake are reminders that people are but visitors in this wilderness.

Along the shore of Sky Pond, the winds blow hard and cold, so picnickers may want to retreat to the protected cove of the Timberline Falls basin. But don't hurry off the mountain. The trip back to the trailhead is a pleasant downhill hike with abundant panoramic views.

11

Bear Lake

DIFFICULTY: nature stroll, handicapped access to lake according to uniform federal accessibility standards, handicapped access with assistance 300 feet in either direction on loop trail
DISTANCE: 0.5-mile loop
USAGE: high
STARTING ELEVATION: 9,475 feet; elevation gain, none
BACKCOUNTRY CAMPSITE: none
SEASON: summer, fall
MAP: USGS 7.5-minute McHenrys Peak

Bear Lake is one of the park's most visited lakes. Its level trail and large parking lot attract huge crowds in the summer. To avoid noise and congestion, hike early. At daybreak, the reflection of peaks on still water is unforgettable, bird songs are uninterrupted by chatter, and the self-guided nature trail can be experienced at a leisurely pace. Spy dew glistening on a web or a hare eating breakfast amid the grass, and Bear Lake will seem a long way from its multi-acre parking lot.

Drive to Bear Lake Road, as described in Hike 1. Follow Bear Lake Road for 9.3 miles to the large parking area at its end. Because this lot is often full by midmorning during the summer, the free park shuttle bus is highly recommended. Parking for the bus is on Bear Lake Road 5.1 miles from its junction with US Highway 36. Schedules are available at visitor centers.

Two booklets enhance the stroll around Bear Lake. The "Bear Lake Nature Trail" pamphlet, published by the Park Service, is an informative guide to plants, wildlife, and geologic features. *The Grandpa Tree* by Mike Donahue is a brief, sensitive, and beautifully illustrated account of the life of a fir tree. Both publications are available at the visitor centers.

Contemplating Longs Peak, Keyboard of the Wind, and Pagoda Peak from Bear Lake

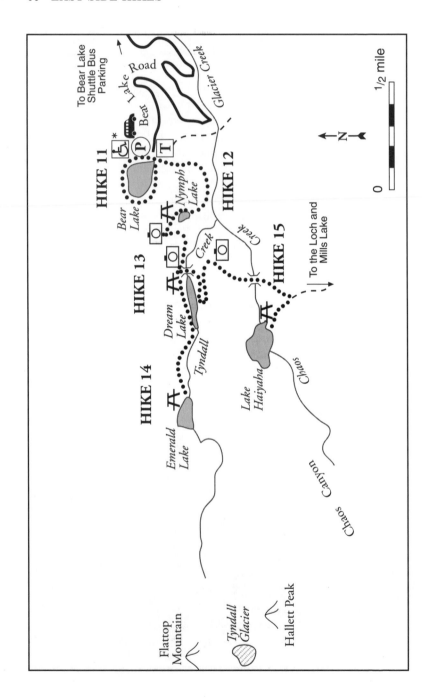

Bear Lake is also a good trail to learn about the park's small mammals and birds. To help children identify Bear Lake inhabitants, several inexpensive guides are available (see Appendix C). Watch for chipmunks, golden-mantled ground squirrels, snowshoe hares, Steller's jays, Clark's nutcrackers, gray jays, blackbilled magpies, chickadees, and hairy woodpeckers. You may even see a harmless green garter snake, the park's only snake.

The Bear Lake Trail is level and very easy to walk. A changing panorama of dramatic peaks rises behind the lake. From the east side, where the hike begins, the sheer north side of Hallett Peak (12,713 feet) is most striking. From the north side of the lake, Longs Peak (14,255 feet), the highest mountain in the park; the spires of the Keyboard of the Winds (west of Longs Peak); and aptly named Pagoda Peak (13,497 feet) dominate. Visible from many trails within the park, these three distinctive peaks are prominent fixtures in the landscape. Getting to know them is like learning the faces of new friends. If you learn their countenances, they greet you on every visit to the park.

On the south side of Bear Lake pass a marshy area where a creek deposits sand and silt that is slowly filling the lake. Each year new soil and new invading plants create a progressively drier environment.

Peer into the lake's waters to catch a glimpse of a greenback cutthroat trout. Overfishing and the introduction of non-native fish almost drove this native trout to extinction. In an effort to save the greenback, the Park Service removed all non-native fish from Bear Lake. As a result, the greenback is making a comeback. To hasten its recovery, fishing is prohibited in Bear Lake. Furthermore, in certain waters in the park, the greenback is protected by a catch-and-release policy, whereby the trout must be returned to the water unharmed. The Park Service hopes that these efforts will restore the greenback to its former numbers.

Despite its name, there are probably no bears in the immediate vicinity of Bear Lake. The lake was named for a black bear sighted during the last century, when the bear population in the region was still vigorous. Rocky Mountain National Park is home now to only a few black bears, perhaps 30 to 40. Hunting and loss of habitat have greatly diminished their numbers.

Loss of bear habitat was accelerated by the Park Service's former fire-suppression policy, which dictated that all forest fires

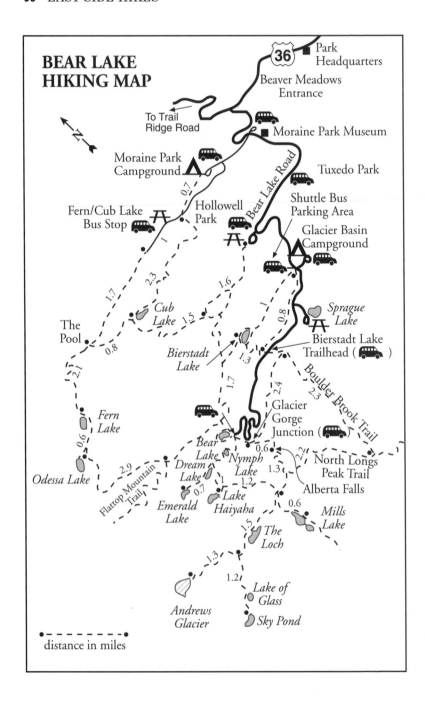

BEAR LAKE HIKING MAP

Park Headquarters

Beaver Meadows Entrance

36

To Trail Ridge Road

Moraine Park Museum

Moraine Park Campground

Tuxedo Park

Bear Lake Road

Fern/Cub Lake Bus Stop

Hollowell Park

Shuttle Bus Parking Area

Glacier Basin Campground

0.7

Cub Lake

Sprague Lake

The Pool

1.7

2.3

1.6

1.5

1

0.8

Bierstadt Lake

Bierstadt Lake Trailhead ( )

0.8

1.3

Boulder Brook Trail

2.1

1.7

2.4

2.3

Fern Lake

Glacier Gorge Junction ( )

0.6

Bear Lake

Nymph Lake

North Longs Peak Trail

2.2

Odessa Lake

2.9

Dream Lake

1.3

Alberta Falls

Flattop Mountain Trail

0.7

1

1.2

0.6

Mills Lake

Emerald Lake

Lake Haiyaha

1.5

The Loch

1.3

1.2

Lake of Glass

Andrews Glacier

Sky Pond

●─ ─ ─ ─ ─●
distance in miles

be promptly extinguished. Lack of naturally occurring fires resulted in loss of meadows, mountain shrub communities, and young forests—habitats where bears find their favorite forage. Without periodic fires, the mosaic of plant communities gave way to expanses of thick forest, which don't support the berries, nutritious forbs, nuts, and grasses that constitute the bulk of a bear's diet. A greater awareness of the positive effects of fire, however, is changing the park's policies to allow most naturally occurring fires to burn themselves out. In addition, recent prescribed burns by the Park Service have increased the variety of habitats. Perhaps with the opening of meadows and shrublands by these fires, the black bear population will rebound.

HIKING OPTIONS:

Bear Lake is the departure point for numerous hikes of every level of difficulty. Use of the park shuttle bus increases your options. See the Bear Lake Hiking Map on page 98.

──────────────── **12** ────────────────

Nymph Lake

DIFFICULTY: easy
DISTANCE: 0.5 mile one way
USAGE: high
STARTING ELEVATION: 9,475 feet; elevation gain,
        225 feet
BACKCOUNTRY CAMPSITE: none
SEASON: summer, fall
MAP: USGS 7.5-minute McHenrys Peak

Nymph Lake is a lovely, lily-covered lake set beneath high peaks. The views from the lake are varied and awe-inspiring, yet its shoreline offers intimate and accessible exploring. Because of its beauty and nearness to the trailhead, Nymph Lake is often crowded. Hike early in the day to have this jewel to yourself. Another benefit of early morning hikes is a near-perfect reflection of towering peaks in the lake's still water.

Nymph Lake

Begin at the Bear Lake Trailhead (see Hike 11). Before the trail arrives at Bear Lake, turn left (south) at the well-marked trail junction. Shortly the trail forks again; keep right, heading uphill. Fir and spruce give way to a towering stand of lodgepole pines along the steep half mile up to Nymph Lake.

The trail meets Nymph Lake at the south end and travels around the eastern shore to the north side of the lake. From the northeastern shore, enjoy an excellent view of precipitous Hallett Peak (12,713 feet), towering more than 3,000 feet above the lake. Looking south from the north side of the lake, Longs Peak, the Keyboard of the Winds, and Pagoda Peak dominate the scene.

Nymph Lake was named for the yellow pond lilies that cover much of this small lake. The lily's scientific name was originally *Nymphaea polysepala*—hence Nymph Lake. The plant's botanical name, though not the lake's, was subsequently changed. From late June through August, large bright yellow blossoms adorn the lily pads. Native Americans once gathered the large seeds of the pond lilies; when roasted, they taste remarkably like popcorn. Today, ducks enjoy the seeds with little competition.

HIKING OPTIONS:

(1) Dream Lake is only 0.6 mile farther and 200 feet higher than Nymph Lake (see Hike 13). (2) Emerald Lake is 1.3 miles farther and 380 feet higher (see Hike 14). (3) Lake Haiyaha is 1.6 miles farther and 520 feet higher (see Hike 15). For more Bear Lake hikes, see the Bear Lake Hiking Map on page 98.

13

Dream Lake

DIFFICULTY: easy
DISTANCE: 1.1 miles one way
USAGE: high
STARTING ELEVATION: 9,475 feet; elevation gain,
    425 feet
BACKCOUNTRY CAMPSITE: none
SEASON: summer, fall
MAP: USGS 7.5-minute McHenrys Peak

Dream Lake is the second in a series of pretty lakes above Bear Lake. The trail is scenic, affording panoramic views as it climbs above Nymph Lake. Dream Lake is well worth a visit in fall, when aspens grace the trail with gold. In summer, hike very early to avoid the crowds who have discovered this trail to be one of the easiest and most pleasing in the park.

The hike begins at the Bear Lake Trailhead (see Hike 11). Hike to Nymph Lake, as described in Hike 12. The trail, which ends just before Nymph Lake, begins again on the west side of the lake. A view to the right, over a rocky ledge, reveals Bear Lake and the ridge of Bierstadt Moraine. The trail soon climbs to an overlook above Nymph Lake. Ahead, Hallett Peak presents a very imposing profile.

In the fall, this section of trail is ablaze with brilliant aspens, whose delicate leaves turn a bright yellow or red. The small rounded leaves flicker in the breeze, creating lively patterns of light on the trail. Because of the way the leaf is attached to the stem, it quakes or trembles, true to the tree's botanical name, *Populus tremuloides,* or trembling aspen.

In the summer, wildflowers are particularly colorful along this slope. Look for Indian paintbrush, which looks like a shaggy brush dipped in vivid vermillion, and purple larkspur, a lovely wild relative of the garden delphinium that is highly poisonous to cattle.

The trail levels a bit and soon presents breathtaking views of Longs Peak and Glacier Basin. Enjoy the view for a quarter mile as the trail traverses the sunny south-facing slope—a magnificent stretch of trail in any season.

Listen for the sound of Tyndall Creek, which flows below, just out of sight. The trail meets this clear running creek, generated in part by glacial runoff from Tyndall Glacier, just before Dream Lake. At the creek the trail divides; the left branch heads over a bridge to Lake Haiyaha (see Hike 15). Keep right for Dream Lake.

Dream Lake is long and narrow, with outstanding reflections of Hallett Peak and the spires of Flattop Mountain. Anglers may be trying for cutthroat trout in its cold waters. Large rocks and logs along the shore make good picnic and viewing spots. Arrive in the morning, when the water is still and hikers are few, for breakfast in a magnificent setting.

Following a lush and beautifully flowered trail, be sure to walk along the north side of the lake to its western end to see where Tyndall Creek flows into the lake.

HIKING OPTIONS:
(1) Emerald Lake is 0.7 mile from and 180 feet higher than Dream Lake (see Hike 14). (2) Lake Haiyaha is 1 mile from and 320 feet above Dream Lake (see Hike 15). For an overview of Bear Lake hikes, see the Bear Lake Hiking Map on page 98.

14

Emerald Lake

DIFFICULTY: moderate
DISTANCE: 1.8 miles one way
USAGE: high
STARTING ELEVATION: 9,475 feet; elevation gain,
    605 feet
BACKCOUNTRY CAMPSITE: none
SEASON: summer, fall
MAP: USGS 7.5-minute McHenrys Peak

Emerald Lake is third in the string of beautiful tarns above Bear Lake. All the lakes are very accessible and, consequently, show signs of overuse. The trail to Emerald Lake, however, is lovely and varied, and crowds can be avoided by starting early in the day. The early-morning hiker is richly rewarded with panoramic views and first-rate reflections of glacier-studded mountains in three very different lakes—Nymph, Dream, and Emerald. It is worthwhile to follow the trail to its conclusion, for Emerald Lake is perhaps the wildest, most dramatic, and most beautifully desolate of the three.

Hike to Dream Lake, as described in Hike 13. Continue on the trail along the north side of Dream Lake. Bright pink elephanthead thrives along this moist section of trail. This plant resembles a totem pole of elephant heads, each with an upturned trunk. At the lake's end, the trail heads steeply up through mature subalpine forest, keeping within sight of Tyndall Creek on the left. Subalpine fir and Engelmann spruce border the trail, with a colorful undergrowth of flowers such as white mountain figwort and blue chimingbells. The climb is steep, gaining over 200 feet in a quarter mile.

Finally, the trail levels and then descends slightly to Emerald Lake. The steep rock walls of Hallett Peak and Flattop Mountain rise directly from the water. Emerald Lake is a tarn, a small lake lying in a basin carved by a glacier that scooped out rocks and carried them down the mountain. Melting snow and glacial runoff then filled the resulting hole with water, thereby creating the lake. The chill winds that blow across the water serve as reminders that this lake is glacier-created and glacier-fed.

Not surprisingly, Emerald Lake is barren. The gray rock that surrounds the lake is broken only by weather-beaten, wind-sculpted limber pines and, occasionally, by hardy firs and spruce. The twisted forms of the pines seem to grow straight from the rock.

Emerald Lake was named for its intense, radiant green waters. On a cloudless day (the best chances are in the morning) the combination of the intensely blue Colorado sky and the luminous green water are strikingly beautiful.

The wildlife is friendly at Emerald Lake. On the rocky slopes, look for yellow-bellied marmots, which are especially abundant on sunny summer days. Picnickers will undoubtedly be visited by golden-mantled ground squirrels, chipmunks, Clark's nutcrackers, Steller's jays, and mountain chickadees. Please do not feed them.

Explore the rocky lake shore with care, following it all the way around to the far (west) side of the lake. At the far side of the lake is a waterfall where water flows down from Tyndall Glacier into Emerald Lake. Use extreme caution, for slippery, unstable snowfields remain throughout the summer on the western shore.

HIKING OPTIONS:

Back at Dream Lake, a trail leads south 1 mile to Lake Haiyaha (elevation gain, 320 feet; see Hike 15). For an overview of Bear Lake hikes, see the Bear Lake Hiking Map on page 98.

15

Lake Haiyaha

DIFFICULTY: moderate
DISTANCE: 2.1 miles one way
USAGE: high
STARTING ELEVATION: 9,475 feet; elevation gain,
    745 feet
BACKCOUNTRY CAMPSITE: none
SEASON: summer, fall
MAP: USGS 7.5-minute McHenrys Peak

Lake Haiyaha is a distinctive lake with stark, boulder-strewn shores. The trail to the lake is very scenic, with wildflowers in the summer, bright foliage in autumn, and a wealth of panoramic vistas in all seasons.

Begin this hike at the Bear Lake Trailhead (see Hike 11). Hike to Dream Lake, as described in Hike 13. At 1 mile from the trailhead, just before arriving at Dream Lake, the trail to Lake Haiyaha heads left. Before continuing, however, walk a short distance up the Emerald Lake Trail, on the right, to visit lovely Dream Lake. After visiting the lake and taking in the bright wildflowers on the path around its north side, backtrack to the Lake Haiyaha junction. The trail heads southwest and crosses a bridge over Tyndall Creek. Lake Haiyaha is 1 mile away.

After the bridge, the trail curves to the right and switchbacks up a shady ridge with a good view of Dream Lake. Snow lasts here into midsummer under the subalpine firs and Engelmann spruce. If there are other hikers at Dream Lake, you may notice how easily voices carry up the mountain. In consideration of other visitors, be aware of the excellent acoustics of natural amphitheaters and control the noise level of your youngsters accordingly.

The trail is moderately steep, but excellent vistas appear as it rounds a bend and climbs an east-facing slope. From the

Rocky shore of Lake Haiyaha

mountainside, Estes Park is visible in the distance. Nearby are good views of Nymph and Bear Lakes. Looking farther down Bear Lake Road, Sprague Lake is also visible. There are also magnificent views to the southeast of Longs Peak, with Mills Lake at its base.

The trail then descends to a forest of fir and spruce, crossing a bridge over Chaos Creek, which flows out of Lake Haiyaha. Approximately 0.2 mile before reaching the lake, the trail from the Loch (Hike 9) and Mills Lake (Hike 8) enters from the south. After this junction, the trail to Lake Haiyaha turns west and leads to a small pond with a beach at its eastern end. The clear, still pond is a lovely place to pause. Large boulders punctuate the shore, looking like moored ships whose "helms" can be seized by nimble youngsters.

The trail continues to the right of the pond over a very rocky landscape, soon disappearing among the boulders. As you head toward a large, handsome limber pine whose twisting limbs reveal its struggle, Lake Haiyaha comes into view.

Large, clear, and beautiful, the lake is wholly surrounded by boulders. The name *haiyaha,* in fact, comes from an Indian word meaning "rock." The large rocks make exploration of the shoreline difficult, but with a little effort, you can travel around the edge of the lake. The other side of the lake offers good views to Longs Peak.

Above the lake to the left is Chaos Canyon, between the high peaks of Otis (to the south) and Hallett (to the north). The impassable jumble of rocks leaves no question as to the origin of this canyon's name.

HIKING OPTIONS:

A hike to Lake Haiyaha can be combined with Glacier Gorge hikes, such as to the Loch and Mills Lake. The park shuttle can be used to return to the Bear Lake Trailhead. See the Bear Lake Hiking Map on page 98.

16

Bierstadt Lake

DIFFICULTY: easy
DISTANCE: 3-mile loop
USAGE: moderate
STARTING ELEVATION: 9,475 feet; elevation gain,
      255 feet
BACKCOUNTRY CAMPSITE: none
SEASON: summer, fall
MAP: USGS 7.5-minute Longs Peak, McHenrys Peak

This easy hike offers exquisite hiking in three very different environments: shady forest, a pristine lake basin, and the side of a steep glacial moraine. The scenery runs from intimate to expansive. The lake, conveniently located at the midpoint of the trail, makes a wonderful picnic spot.

This hike begins at the Bear Lake Trailhead and ends at the Bierstadt Lake Trailhead. Use two cars or the shuttle bus to connect the trailheads. You can park at the shuttle parking area or at the smaller lots at either trailhead. All three are on Bear Lake Road. To reach these lots, drive to Bear Lake Road, as described in Hike 11. The shuttle parking area is 5.1 miles from the junction with US Highway 36. Limited parking is available at the Bierstadt Lake and Bear Lake Trailheads, at 6.6 miles and 9.3 miles from the junction.

Head right (north) on the Bear Lake Trail (Hike 11) and shortly come to the Flattop Mountain Trail on the right. Take this trail and begin a fairly steep ascent through pines and aspens. As you climb, observe the tenacity of the trailside trees, which appear to rise right out of the boulders beside the trail.

At 0.4 mile, arrive at a second fork and again bear right. The trail now travels along the top of Bierstadt Moraine, which leads toward Bierstadt Lake. Numerous ground squirrels accompany you on this part of the hike; resist the temptation to feed these bold beggars.

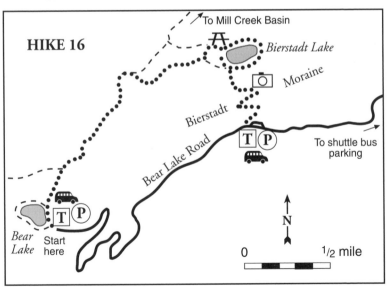

The ascent is quickly rewarded by outstanding views of impressive peaks, including the dramatic profiles of Hallett Peak (12,713 feet) and Flattop Mountain (12,324 feet). After 0.75 mile, the Bierstadt Lake Trail forks. Take the right fork, which descends gently into the cool, shady tranquility of a mature forest of Engelmann spruce and subalpine fir, where sufficient light filters through the branches to dispel any gloom. At this point, the trail improves, becoming wider, smoother, and more level.

Within this magnificent subalpine forest, you can sense the passing of generations—the millennium of trees that have lived and died here. Weathered trunks of tremendous lodgepole pines lying on the forest floor are mute reminders of the trees that once dominated the area but were long ago shaded out by the firs and spruce. Now the fallen pines tell of the natural succession of trees in the forest. The downed trees provide natural benches for a snack stop, places to play "King of the Limb," or balance beams on which children can test their skills.

Don't rush through this area too quickly. Rest on a great trunk or boulder, watch the acrobatic chipmunks, or browse the sculpture garden of giant gnarled upturned roots. Shortly, there is another fork in the trail. As the sign indicates, take the trail to the left.

At 1.5 miles from Bear Lake, come to the Bierstadt Lake fork. A spur trail on the right leads to the water, where mallards provide a noisy welcome. The large rocks scattered along the shoreline invite resting, reading, or playing. Take time to gaze upon the profiles of Longs Peak, Hallett Peak, and Flattop Mountain, which create the exquisite backdrop for the 1.4-acre lake.

This is a perfect picnic spot. The lake has several pebbly beaches where tiny waves lap teasingly. Explore the shoreline on an overgrown footpath. The most difficult part of the hike is over; the trail is literally all downhill from here.

A short section of trail at the lake's southwest end leads to the main trail, where you head left. (Or, if you wish to retrace your steps to Bear Lake, return to the main trail the way you came, turn left at the main trail, and keep to the left, heading south.) Travel on a straight path through a tremendous stand of lodgepole pines, whose slim, straight trunks rise row after row. Indians once used the tall pines as tepee poles—hence the tree's name. The forest rapidly thins as the trail approaches the edge of the Bierstadt

Mallard on Bierstadt Lake

Moraine, where you are suddenly greeted with a wide view of the mountains to the south and east, as well as of the valley below. The transformation in scenery is dramatic and renewing. The views of the Front Range are truly magnificent. Below, Glacier Creek winds through the green valley.

The hillside is pleasant as well. In midsummer, wildflowers are abundant, and in fall the golden foliage of the aspens is spectacular. Ponderosa pines grow on the moraine in open parklike stands. The pines are trees out of a child's imagination, perfectly formed giants with huge cones and bark that smells like vanilla.

The trail down the moraine is hot and sunny on most summer days. You will be glad to be descending as you pass many hot and grumbling hikers struggling up the path. Following the descent of the moraine, return briefly to a level, shady path, after a short distance arriving at Bierstadt Lake Trailhead and the completion of your hike.

HIKING OPTIONS:
    See the Bear Lake Hiking Map on page 98.

—————————————— **17** ——————————————

Flattop Mountain

DIFFICULTY: strenuous
DISTANCE: 4.4 miles one way
USAGE: high
STARTING ELEVATION: 9,475 feet; elevation gain,
    2,849 feet
BACKCOUNTRY CAMPSITE: none
SEASON: summer, fall
MAP: USGS 7.5-minute McHenrys Peak

Flattop Mountain is a superb hike, strenuous but rewarding in a multitude of ways. The views from the trail and summit are outstanding. Wildlife is frequently seen, and wildflowers in midsummer are spectacular. Best of all, the well-trod path is so smooth that you can spend most of your time watching the wonders around you instead of watching your feet.

Begin at the Bear Lake Trailhead (see Hike 11). Head right (north) on the Bear Lake Trail and, after a short distance, turn right and head uphill on an unpaved path marked by a trail sign for Flattop Mountain. The trail climbs steeply and quickly above Bear Lake among aspens, which are particularly beautiful in the fall. After 0.4 mile, the trail divides. The right fork leads to Bierstadt Lake (Hike 16). Keep left and continue to climb. After a few switchbacks, enjoy good views of Longs Peak to the south and Bear Lake below.

After another 0.4 mile, the trail divides again. Take the left fork. The Flattop Mountain Trail rises steeply through fir and spruce. Beginning here, enjoy good views through breaks in the trees. Dream Lake Overlook, on the left, is a good place to see how far you've come. There are also excellent views to the southeast of Longs Peak with lovely Mills Lake below it. Angular Hallett Peak looms overhead to the west.

As treeline approaches, the trees become sparse and stunted. "Banner trees," with branches growing on only the east side of the trunk, reveal the force of the prevailing westerly winds. Only the limbs on the leeward side have escaped the wind's destructive and

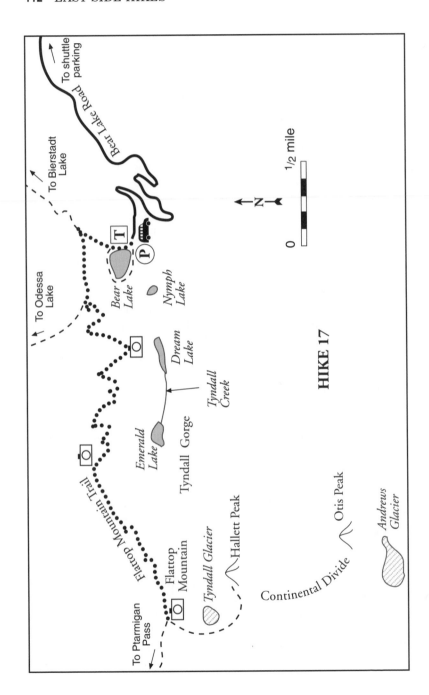

To shuttle parking

Bear Lake Road

To Bierstadt Lake

To Odessa Lake

T

P

Bear Lake

Nymph Lake

Dream Lake

Tyndall Creek

Emerald Lake

Tyndall Gorge

Flattop Mountain Trail

Flattop Mountain

Tyndall Glacier

Hallett Peak

To Ptarmigan Pass

Continental Divide

Otis Peak

Andrews Glacier

N

0   ½ mile

HIKE 17

Ranger-led hike on Flattop Mountain

scouring blasts. At treeline, the gnarled islands of *krummholz* (a German word meaning "crooked wood") struggle against the high winds, intense cold, and short growing season.

Above treeline, the views are stupendous. There are also marvelous sights on the tundra beneath your feet. A multitude of minute but vibrant wildflowers stand out like jewels against the gray rock. Look for the Colorado blue columbine, a showy flower with blue sepals and white petals. It is the Colorado state flower and was once abundant throughout these mountains, before acquisitive and selfish hikers drastically reduced its numbers. Park regulations now prohibit the picking of wildflowers.

Look also among the rocks for pikas and marmots. The elusive and industrious pika, a round-eared relative of the rabbit, resembles a guinea pig. During the summer, it busily scurries over the rocks, gathering flowers and grasses. The pika lays its harvest of herbs on rocks to dry and then gathers and piles the hay in little stacks. The pika assaults this chore with unceasing energy, for these piles will be its food during the long alpine winter. The animal's ability to scamper with speed and precision is due to the "nonskid" fur on the soles of its feet.

Watch also for the larger and more easily observed yellow-bellied marmot. On sunny days, this relative of the woodchuck can usually be found sunning itself on the rocks. Like the pika, the marmot also dens on talus slopes and boulder-covered mountainsides. Unlike the hard-working pika, the objective of the indolent marmot is to acquire a sufficient amount of body fat to see it through its winter's hibernation. By summer's end, most marmots have sleek coats and pleasingly plump figures.

Watch closely also for the well-camouflaged ptarmigan, a grouse that inhabits the alpine tundra. In summer you may see a mottled brown hen with chicks.

The trail steadily climbs to the top of aptly named Flattop Mountain, whose summit is a spacious, uplifted plateau. Extending from Bighorn Flats to Andrews Glacier, this high plain was once continuous with the broad plateau of Trail Ridge, which is visible to the north and now separated from Flattop Mountain by Forest Canyon.

The summit, though not dramatic, is a fine place to be. The broad expanse of Flattop allows hikers to spread out in every direction, and the views are spectacular.

HIKING OPTIONS:

(1) An easy 0.3-mile trail leads south from Flattop Mountain to the top of Tyndall Glacier. The trail is clearly marked by cairns and signs. (2) A very challenging trail that gains 389 feet in 0.6 mile leads to Hallett Peak, one of the most dramatic summits in the park. Follow the trail leading south across the summit of Flattop, past Tyndall Glacier. The path periodically disappears among rocks, but cairns point the way. The way is steep and the rocks unstable, so climb slowly and carefully. The views from the summit at 12,713 feet are spectacular.

18

Gem Lake

DIFFICULTY: moderate
DISTANCE: 1.8 miles one way from Twin Owls Trailhead;
    2 miles one way from Gem Lake Trailhead
USAGE: high
STARTING ELEVATION: 7,920 feet (Twin Owls
    Trailhead), 7,740 feet (Gem Lake Trailhead);
    elevation gain, 910 feet from Twin Owls Trailhead,
    1,090 feet from Gem Lake Trailhead
BACKCOUNTRY CAMPSITE: none
SEASON: summer, fall
MAP: USGS 7.5-minute Estes Park

This delightful hike among the weird and wonderful rock formations of Lumpy Ridge offers beautiful views, diverse vegetation,
and a child-sized lake. In summer, however, the trail can be hot
and tiring and a real challenge for youngsters. To combat fatigue
on this worthwhile hike, start early in the morning; bring plenty
of drinks, hats, and sunscreen; and proceed slowly.

From the intersection of US Bypass 34 and MacGregor Avenue on the north side of Estes Park, turn right (north) onto
MacGregor Avenue, which becomes Devils Gulch Road north of
this intersection. Drive 0.8 mile on Devils Gulch Road to
MacGregor Ranch. Turn in the driveway for the ranch and continue to the parking lot at the end of the road, a distance of 0.8
mile. The Twin Owls Trailhead is at the east end of the parking
lot. To reach the Gem Lake Trailhead, continue on Devils Gulch
Road 0.75 mile past the MacGregor Ranch. The trailhead is at a
parking lot on the left side of the road.

The preferred route to Gem Lake is from the Twin Owls
Trailhead. This route is shorter and gains less elevation. If the
parking lot at the Twin Owls Trailhead is full, use the Gem Lake
trailhead. From the Gem Lake Trailhead, the well-marked trail

Bear Lake

crosses private land through meadows for 0.5 mile, then climbs a series of switchbacks to the junction with the trail from Twin Owls Trailhead, 0.8 mile from the Gem Lake Trailhead. Keep right (east) at the junction.

The trail at Twin Owls starts under a prominent rock formation that, especially from a distance, looks like two owls. Lumpy Ridge is a popular spot for rock climbers. Both the National Park and the Colorado Mountain School of Estes Park run introductory rock-climbing programs here. (For more information on rock climbing, see Chapter 1.)

From the Twin Owls Trailhead, hike through a stand of young aspens and then begin the climb up the ridge. Ponderosa pines dot the slopes, framing but not obscuring the excellent views of Longs Peak and Estes Park. These pines are home to Abert's squirrels. These beautiful and distinctive squirrels are dark gray or black, with conspicuous ear tufts and a long, full tail fringed with white hairs.

Notice the many dead ponderosa pines. They have been invaded and killed by the mountain pine beetle. Most of the trees have numerous holes made by woodpeckers. These holes provide homes for swallows, chickadees, bluebirds, nuthatches, and other cavity dwelling birds.

Also along the trail are sun-loving wildflowers and an abundance of prickly pear cactus. Local Indians used this cactus in a variety of ways, one of which was to treat the mumps by removing the spines, roasting the stems, and tying the cactus to the patient's neck.

As the trail turns left to climb a gulch between Lumpy Ridge and a second, smaller ridge, it suddenly enters a cooler, moister environment where Douglas fir thrives among flowers and shrubs. As the trail climbs up and over the ridge, sun and wind return, and Douglas fir gives way to limber pine, which survives tremendous adversity. At treeline, high winds often twist limber pine into beautiful gnarled shapes. The limber pine is the only conifer in Rocky Mountain National Park whose needles grow in bunches of five.

The trail shortly meets the trail from the Gem Lake Trailhead, which enters on the right. Immediately after this junction, good

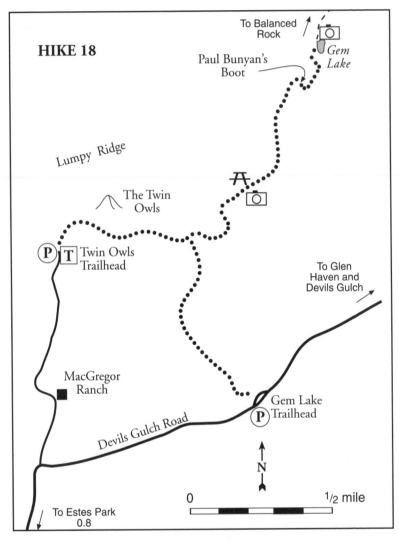

HIKE 18

To Balanced Rock

Gem Lake

Paul Bunyan's Boot

Lumpy Ridge

The Twin Owls

P T Twin Owls Trailhead

To Glen Haven and Devils Gulch

MacGregor Ranch

Gem Lake
P Trailhead

Devils Gulch Road

N

0   1/2 mile

To Estes Park
0.8

views are abundant and the picnicking and rock-scrambling spots are too attractive to resist. In several places, spur trails lead to overlooks. If the group is weary of hiking, this spot makes a satisfying turnaround point.

Farther up the trail are more unusual rock formations, in which imaginative children (and adults) can see Gila monsters, chickens, snakes, and, in one amusing pile, two turtles lying on a whale. The rock faces of numerous ghoulish unnameables watch from the ridgetop or emerge from the surfaces of fallen boulders. The rocks also can be forts, lookouts, ancient beached ships, and trolls' caves. Only your imagination limits what you see on Lumpy Ridge.

Good views continue after an aspen grove until the trail turns into a cool, moist canyon. Enjoy the sudden wealth of flowers thriving there. In autumn there is an abundance of wild raspberries and bitter golden currants. Native Americans mixed the currants with dried buffalo meat and fat and poured the mixture into bags to form loaves. Closer to our modern tastes, settlers made a tasty currant jam with the addition of much sugar and spice.

Shortly after leaving the canyon, hike up a series of switchbacks to Paul Bunyan's Boot, one of the more famous of Lumpy Ridge's rock formations. The hole in the sole of the boot was created naturally by chemical weathering. Look for other interesting rock formations in this area and on the ridges above you.

Leaving this natural sculpture garden, climb by another series of switchbacks to tiny Gem Lake, which is only 0.2 acre and 5 feet deep. Gem Lake is truly a gem, a lovely place to picnic, play, and rest. Sit on its small sandy beach and contemplate the high rock walls that rise dramatically behind it. When the wind is still they are reflected perfectly in the clear water. The beach will beckon the child in you to remove your shoes and cool your hot, tired feet.

HIKING OPTIONS:

Two miles beyond Gem Lake there is a fascinating rock formation called Balanced Rock, 3.8 miles from the Twin Owls Trailhead. To reach this destination, continue traveling north from the north end of the lake. After 0.5 mile, reach a fork in the trail. Keep left, descending slightly to a second junction in 0.25 mile. Again keep left. This trail leads into a gully containing many interesting formations, including the unmistakable Balanced Rock. From Gem Lake, there is no elevation gain.

19

Deserted Village

DIFFICULTY: moderate
DISTANCE: 3 miles one way
USAGE: low
STARTING ELEVATION: 7,960 feet; elevation gain,
    200 feet
BACKCOUNTRY CAMPSITE: none
SEASON: spring, summer, fall
MAPS: USGS 7.5-minute Glen Haven, Estes Park

This gentle, unassuming trail descends to a canyon and follows the North Fork of the Big Thompson River along a cool and shady path to a meadow that was once the site of a nineteenth-century resort. Today only one cabin remains. The flowers along the path are plentiful, and in late summer ripe berries are abundant. Adventurous children can find spots for swimming in the North Fork on hot summer days. The trail begins in the Roosevelt National Forest, at the park's northeastern boundary. The long drive to the trailhead goes through Devils Gulch, where the winding road drops 600 feet in 1 mile. On the way you pass tiny Glen Haven, a picturesque western town that is a perfect place to stop for a snack.

From Estes Park, find Devils Gulch Road (see Hike 18 for directions) and drive 9 miles (passing the town of Glen Haven) to a dirt road at a sign indicating access to Roosevelt National Forest. This road is 1.9 miles past Glen Haven. Turn left onto the dirt road and follow it 2.2 miles to the parking lot at the road's end. The trailhead is at the southeast end of the parking lot. Heavily used by horse riders, the trail may be littered with manure.

Head over a small rise, and then descend quickly into a cool gulch. Just before reaching the North Fork, the trail forks. Head right for Deserted Village. The trail follows the river, providing plenty of access to the water. Wildflowers and berry bushes line the way for the entire distance. Watch particularly for delicious wild raspberries.

North Fork of the Big Thompson River

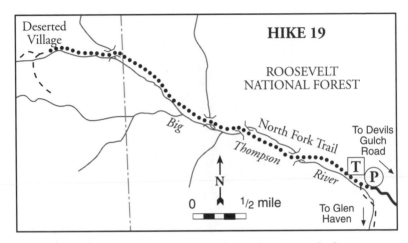

The trail is almost level. A variety of trees including aspen, willow, blue spruce, and Douglas fir appear. Numerous aspens make this a fine hike in the fall, when their leaves turn brilliant gold. Cross and recross the river on a series of bridges as the canyon cliffs rise in interesting formations above you.

After approximately 1 mile, the trail now passes through private property, complete with barbed wire and many buildings, including a large stable. The feeling of wildness is lost, if only temporarily.

After crossing another bridge, follow an old wide, level road for a short distance before the trail reappears. The trail temporarily narrows, then widens again at the national park boundary.

After crossing three more large bridges, arrive at the meadow that was the site of a popular hunting resort founded by the infamous Lord Dunraven in the 1870s. Today a lone cabin is all that remains.

Lord Dunraven was an Irish lord who visited Estes Park in 1872 and was impressed by its magnificent scenery and fine hunting. The wealthy Dunraven made up his mind to buy the entire area for a private hunting preserve. By using and abusing the homestead laws, he accumulated 15,000 acres, mostly under fraudulent claims. Honest and indignant homesteaders eventually discovered his scheme and challenged his claims. Frustrated by the litigation, the aspiring Rocky Mountain lord surrendered his holdings in 1880 and returned to Ireland. His legacy continues in the names of mountains, lakes, and meadows within Rocky Mountain National Park.

Others succeeded Lord Dunraven in running the fashionable hunting resort at this site. Its popularity might have continued, but a dysentery epidemic in 1909 significantly lessened public enthusiasm. By 1914, the resort was abandoned.

20

Bridal Veil Falls

DIFFICULTY: moderate
DISTANCE: 3.2 miles one way
USAGE: low
STARTING ELEVATION: 7,840 feet; elevation gain
    1,060 feet
BACKCOUNTRY CAMPSITE: 1.4 miles from the trailhead
SEASON: spring, summer, fall
MAP: USGS 7.5-minute Estes Park

Escape the crowds for a long but undemanding walk to Bridal Veil Falls. A gentle trail rolls through montane meadows and follows Cow Creek to the tallest falls in the park. Along the way, the anthropomorphic rock formations of Lumpy Ridge loom high above the hiker. Only 1.4 miles from the trailhead, backpackers can find a quiet campsite on Cow Creek. This dry, sunny hike can get quite warm in midsummer, so bring plenty of liquids. Plentiful aspen display excellent color in autumn.

From the intersection of US Bypass 34 and MacGregor Avenue on the north side of Estes Park, turn right (north) onto MacGregor Avenue, which becomes Devils Gulch Road. Drive 3.3 miles on Devils Gulch Road to a dirt road on the left signed for McGraw Ranch. (This is a private road, but the landowners permit the public to use the road to reach the ranch.) Turn left onto the dirt road and drive 2.1 miles to its termination at McGraw Ranch. Park along the side of the road, after the cattle grate, but before the ranch gate. Enter the ranch on foot.

Bridal Veil Falls

This hike begins at the historic Indian Head Ranch, which originally operated as a cattle ranch and later as a dude ranch in the late 1800s. Today the ranch no longer hosts dudes, but provides critical winter grazing for elk and bighorn sheep. Follow a dirt road past the historic cabins to the Cow Creek Trailhead.

At the trailhead, the North Boundary Trail heads right (north) while the Cow Creek Trail follows an old road west. Take the Cow Creek Trail down the old road which parallels the willow-lined creek. Broad, flowered meadows flank the trail, rising to high green slopes on either side. Summer flowers include orange Indian paintbrush, white cut-leaf daisy, yellow blanket flower, and bright pink locoweed.

Locoweed graces the surrounding meadow with beautiful color, but the pretty plant can cause great harm to cattle. The plant absorbs barium from the soil, and if cattle consume a great quantity, the animals may actually suffer poisoning and act crazy. Thus the name "loco," which in Spanish means "crazy."

After about 0.6 mile, the road narrows to a trail and gently climbs. Cow Creek drops away to the left down a steep ravine. Pass through a wet area where wild roses thrive, and then arrive at a trail junction 1.2 miles from the trailhead. To the left lie Gem Lake and Balanced Rock. Take the right fork and continue straight ahead (west). Fragrant ponderosa pines flank the trail. Their cinnamon-colored bark, broken into platelets, resembles a thick giraffe's neck. If you're melting in the hot sun, find a pine and sniff a whiff of butterscotch from its bark. It smells as if cookies are baking inside!

At 1.4 miles from the trailhead, arrive at a turnoff on the left for Rabbit Ears backcountry campsite. High above the trail a rock formation illustrates the source of this colorful name. The campsite is located in a shady area near Cow Creek and is a good site for family backpacking.

The trail continues west, once again traveling beside Cow Creek. Pass many aspen, grazed and scarred by elk, beside the trail. Measure your progress by the rock formations to the right (north) of the trail. Youngsters can find faces and other recognizable shapes in the outcroppings.

At approximately 1.9 miles from the trailhead, arrive at another junction. The trail to the left heads for the Twin Owls parking area. Stay right and begin to climb gently. Rise into the shade of

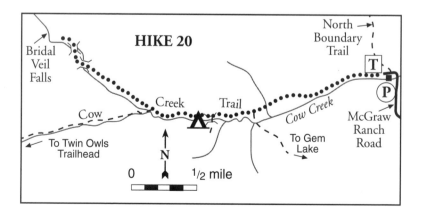

a lodgepole forest. The trail levels and then dodges numerous large and amusing trailside boulders, including a cabin-sized boulder to your right and a shark with a gaping mouth to your left.

Finally arrive at the banks of Cow Creek and some welcome shade and moisture. The remainder of the trail hops along the creek bank, crossing and recrossing the creek, following it upstream to the falls. Just below the falls, hikers must ascend a smooth and steep rock face. The ascent is short, but children might need assistance.

After climbing up a set of stone steps, hikers arrive at Bridal Veil Falls. The impressive falls glides powerfully over rock and bounces upon impact, sending out a lacy veil of spray to onlookers. The cool spot at the falls is excellent for a picnic, a "photo op," or simply a rest stop before you retrace your steps to the trailhead.

21

Deer Mountain

DIFFICULTY: strenuous
DISTANCE: 3 miles one way
USAGE: high
STARTING ELEVATION: 8,930 feet; elevation gain,
    1,083 feet
BACKCOUNTRY CAMPSITE: none
SEASON: summer, fall
MAP: USGS 7.5-minute Estes Park

The trail up Deer Mountain offers wonderful views from sunny, open slopes. From the summit, the whole eastern side of the park is visible. The disadvantage of this hike is that the first section is within sight and sound of busy Deer Ridge Junction and its connecting highways. In addition, horse riders heavily use this trail. An early start on this popular hike will bring you up to the summit before the crowds, traffic, and heat, and will spare you the thunderstorms that arrive most summer afternoons.

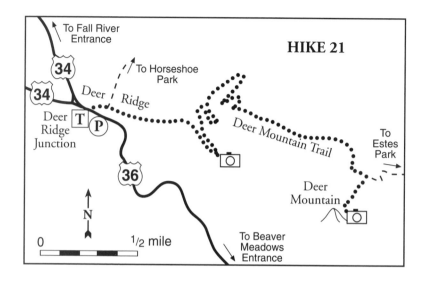

The trailhead is located at Deer Ridge Junction, where US Highways 34 and 36 intersect. The junction is 2.9 miles northwest of the Beaver Meadows Entrance Station. Park along the shoulder of US Highway 36, just east of the junction, at a trail sign for Deer Mountain.

The trail starts on a sunny slope amid ponderosa pines. Bring plenty to drink on this hike, for much of the trail traverses these bright, dry slopes. At the first junction, bear right. The trail to the left descends into Horseshoe Park.

Ascend the sunny slope amid a variety of sun-loving flowers. There are fine views of the Mummy Range to the northwest and the Front Range and Longs Peak to the south and southwest. After reaching a grove of aspens that has been heavily grazed by elk, the trail begins to switchback up the mountain.

The trail traverses to the west side of the mountain, where there is often a cooling wind. The path becomes shadier as it climbs among conifers. The switchbacks are tiring, but the changing views keep the trip interesting. Views alternate between the sheer east face of Ypsilon Mountain (13,514 feet) and the massive square summit of Longs Peak (14,255 feet), the highest in the park.

After a little more than 1 mile, the trail heads to the north side of the mountain. The switchbacks continue, finally leveling off on a broad, flat shoulder of the mountain. Enter an area studded with the dramatic corpses of lightning-struck limber pines. Because of its location, Deer Mountain is a magnet for thunderstorms, which are very frequent in this part of the Rockies. The mountain is struck often, and the resulting fires have created the strange forest of charred statuesque pines that adorns it. If the skies look threatening, retreat to a lower elevation. See precautions set forth in Chapter 1.

Continue on this broad plateau for 0.6 mile to a spur trail on the right. Take this trail, which leads directly to the summit. Do not continue straight ahead because that trail descends steeply to Estes Park.

Once on the spur trail, it is a short hike to the summit. The trail becomes tough at the end, but the summit is soon attained. The summit offers good views and an excellent spot to picnic.

22

Alluvial Fan Trail

DIFFICULTY: nature stroll, handicapped access with
    assistance
DISTANCE: 0.5 mile one way
USAGE: high
STARTING ELEVATION: 8,540 feet; elevation gain, 40 feet
BACKCOUNTRY CAMPSITE: none
SEASON: spring, summer, fall
MAP: USGS 7.5-minute Trail Ridge

The Alluvial Fan Trail tours the dramatic changes wrought by the violent Lawn Lake flood of 1982. When the earthen dam burst at Lawn Lake, 14 miles away, a wall of water 30 feet high crashed down the narrow Roaring River Valley, dislodging hundreds of tons of boulders and uprooting trees. The resulting mass of boulders and debris, which fans out from Horseshoe Falls, creates an eerie and strangely beautiful place. Imagine the force with which the boulders and uprooted trees were hurled through the valley above. Now a gentle paved path winds through the debris fan and across a bridge over the cascading river. The boulders that once

Intrepid young climber on Alluvial Fan Trail

embodied the terrifying force of the flood now form a giant playground for rockhopping youngsters. Try visiting the fan at dusk, when the sun is setting over beautiful Endovalley, and the sky above Horseshoe Park glows in lovely pastels.

Drive to Deer Ridge Junction, as described in Hike 21. At the junction, turn right toward Horseshoe Park on US Highway 34. Drive 1.8 miles to the road to the Endovalley picnic area and turn left. (From the Fall River Entrance Station, the road to Endovalley is 2.1 miles west on US Highway 34.) After the turn for Endovalley, the Alluvial Fan Trail is 0.5 mile on your right. Parking is at the trailhead.

The immense volume of water and debris unleashed by the dam redesigned Horseshoe Park. The lake across the road was created when flood material dammed the Fall River. The destructive force of the flood was immense; three campers lost their lives, $31 million in property was destroyed, and muddy flood water stood 6 feet deep in the streets of Estes Park. For more information on the flood, pick up the Park Service brochure "The Flood of '82," which is available at park visitor centers.

Notice the numerous dead trees standing amid the fan's boulders. Debris carried by the flood choked the trees' root systems. During the summer, these trees are home to a population of birds, including swallows, sapsuckers, flickers, and hairy woodpeckers.

The lake across the road is an excellent place for children to explore. Its wide gravel shores are especially inviting for walking and picnicking. Unfortunately, the lake is not accessible to wheelchairs or strollers.

23

Beaver Boardwalk

DIFFICULTY: nature stroll, handicapped access according
    to uniform federal accessibility standards
DISTANCE: 0.25-mile loop
USAGE: high
STARTING ELEVATION: 8,600 feet; elevation gain, none
BACKCOUNTRY CAMPSITE: none
SEASON: spring, summer, fall
MAP: USGS 7.5-minute Trail Ridge

Stroll along the Beaver Boardwalk to see how beavers can change a landscape and create new and fertile environments for diverse plants and animals. The wide wooden boardwalk crosses a series of ponds and marshes among beaver dams and lodges. Although most of the beavers have left the site, this stroll above the water is always lively with birds, insects, and occasional deer. Children love looking down into the clear water of the ponds to see trout, ducks, and aquatic insects.

Drive to Deer Ridge Junction, as described in Hike 21. Turn left on US Highway 34 and drive 1.9 miles to the Beaver Boardwalk parking area, on the right (north) side of the road.

The stroll begins among a variety of trees, including Engelmann spruce, subalpine fir, lodgepole pine, and aspen. After a

Beaver Boardwalk

brief walk though the trees, the wooden boardwalk, which is accessible to strollers and wheelchairs, leads over a marshy area to ponds created by beaver dams. The boardwalk meanders over the water for 0.25 mile. Informative signs along the way help you to interpret what you see. Watch for the mallards and other ducks that make their nests in these ponds.

The ponds at the Beaver Boardwalk were created by numerous beaver dams along the Hidden Valley Creek. Before the beavers arrived, Hidden Valley Creek probably coursed through a grassy meadow. A series of beaver dams along the creek inhibited the flow and caused it to overflow its banks, creating shallow ponds. Beavers build dams in order to provide quiet water for food gathering and safe haven for their lodges. Dams raise and stabilize the water level so that the lodges, whose entrances are below water, can be built in the center of creeks. This location discourages most predators from invading the beavers' homes. The living quarters of the lodges are cozy and dry because they are built above the water level of the river. Dusk and dawn are the best times to look for beaver and other wildlife at the ponds.

24

Mummy Range

DIFFICULTY: strenuous
DISTANCE: Mount Chapin, 1.5 miles; Mount Chiquita, 2.4
      miles; Ypsilon Mountain, 3.5 miles—all one way
USAGE: low
STARTING ELEVATION: 10,640 feet; elevation gain, 1,814
      feet to Mount Chapin; 2,429 feet to Mount Chiquita;
      2,874 feet to Ypsilon Mountain
BACKCOUNTRY CAMPSITE: none
SEASON: summer, fall
MAP: USGS 7.5-minute Trail Ridge

The peaks of the Mummy Range make memorable, though very demanding, destinations. The summit views from all three peaks are unforgettable, and the hikes have a wildness that is rare in

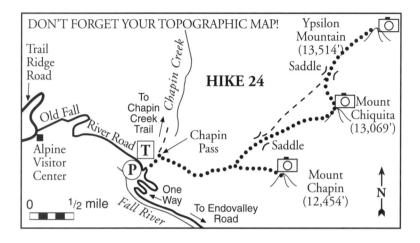

this well-visited park. There are, however, no trails up the steep and rocky slopes. To add to the difficulty, the starting elevation is high and the elevation gain significant. Yet hiking on the flower-filled slopes of the Mummies is an adventure, and a hike of any length is worthwhile. The Chapin Creek drainage is filled with deer and elk, and the scenery is filled with grandeur. Hikers of all ages and abilities can walk this hike to the flowered meadows near Chapin Pass, but only experienced young hikers, with their parents, should attempt to reach the peaks.

Drive to Deer Ridge Junction, as described in Hike 21. Turn right at the junction and proceed 1.8 miles to Endovalley Road. Turn left at Endovalley Road and drive 2 miles until the pavement ends. Old Fall River Road starts here. Drive up Old Fall River Road for 6.3 miles to the sign for the Chapin Creek Trailhead (Marker 20), on the right side of the road. Parking is available along the road. (From the Fall River Entrance Station, Endovalley Road is 2.1 miles west on US Highway 34.) Because Old Fall River Road is one-way, you must return via Trail Ridge Road, which is 2.4 miles from the trailhead.

The trail begins on a wide path ascending through subalpine fir and spruce. Follow this path uphill for 200 yards to Chapin Pass, where a narrow signed trail heads right (east) toward Mount Chapin.

The trail leads through a wet area filled in the summer with wildflowers. Look for red Indian paintbrush, white mountain bistort, and purple and yellow composites. Pass a small pond that may have deer and elk tracks on its shore. Although similar, elk tracks are approximately 4½ by 3 inches, while deer tracks are only 3 by 2¾ inches and are more heart-shaped.

The trail heads steeply up a ridge. Among the rocks, watch for beautiful Colorado blue columbine, a striking flower of white petals and sky blue sepals. Pause on this ridge to look down to the verdant valleys of Chapin Creek and Cache la Poudre River. The valleys are excellent deer and elk habitat. Arrive in the early morning to see them.

The faint trail winds around the southern side of a bulge on the ridge and leads to treeline. Before the trees completely disappear, the trail passes sprawling islands of *krummholz,* also known as elfinwood. These shrublike trees struggle to survive in

Tundra hiking on Mount Chiquita

the face of severe temperatures, gale winds, and destructive snow and ice. Dead trees on the windward sides of the gnarled tree islands protect the living growth in the center and on the leeward side. Look carefully for deer and elk in this area.

Above treeline, pick up the faint trail that traverses the west-facing slope of Mount Chapin, the mountain farthest to the right. At 12,454 feet, Mount Chapin is the nearest and the smallest of the three peaks. If it is your goal, simply head upslope toward the summit. Mount Chapin offers a view down its precipitous south-facing wall to dramatic rock spires. The best view, however, is from the higher, eastern summit.

If Mount Chiquita (13,069 feet) is your destination, traverse Mount Chapin on a faint trail, crossing its west slope, heading north to the saddle between the two peaks. Unstable talus slopes and deep tundra turf impede progress. From the saddle, at 12,000 feet, pick a route northeast to the top of Mount Chiquita. The 1,000-foot climb to the summit is demanding and requires more time than you might suspect. Unstable rocks again slow progress. From Mount Chiquita's summit, however, a truly spectacular panoramic view opens up, including a breathtaking peek down Chiquita's sheer east face. A good map will help you to identify the universe of mountains, lakes, and valleys spread before you.

To climb Ypsilon Mountain (13,514 feet), descend Chiquita to the saddle and then ascend to Ypsilon's summit. Alternatively, skip the summit of Chiquita altogether. Instead, traverse its western side for 1 mile to reach the aforementioned saddle. Both routes are very demanding. Traversing these mountains is much harder than it looks. The slopes are steep, and travel across the trailless tundra is tiring. From the lofty summit of Ypsilon Mountain, the 360-degree view is sensational. Look down the sheer east face for a striking view of Spectacle Lakes, more than 2,000 feet below.

The variety of tundra wildflowers on all these slopes is astounding. From early to midsummer, watch for the alpine forget-me-not, a minute flower of the most intense blue. Larger and more common throughout the summer are the Rydbergia, or old-man-of-the mountain. These yellow flowers always face east, away from the prevailing westerly winds. Their peculiar name derives from the whitish hairs that cover leaves and stems to protect against cold and dehydration. The flowers of the alpine tundra have adapted to what is among the severest terrestrial habitats for plants. Their size reflects the limitations of plant growth at these altitudes.

Return to the trailhead by traversing back across the mountain slopes. Or descend a few hundred feet into the green valley above Chapin Creek and hike south to Chapin Pass. The walk below treeline is easier, and the chance of seeing deer is excellent. Be sure not to descend too far into the valley, thus adding unnecessary climbing to your already strenuous hike.

25

Lily Mountain

DIFFICULTY: moderate
DISTANCE: 1.5 miles one way
USAGE: moderate
STARTING ELEVATION: 8,780 feet; elevation gain,
    1,006 feet
BACKCOUNTRY CAMPSITE: none
SEASON: summer, fall
MAP: USGS 7.5-minute Longs Peak

At 9,786 feet, Lily Mountain is hardly monumental, but its summit provides impressive and memorable views. Because the trail is relatively short and only moderately difficult, an ascent of Lily Mountain is an excellent first climb for young and aspiring mountaineers. Its trailhead is also convenient to Estes Park. The only drawback to this trail is that, owing to its proximity to Colorado State Highway 7, vehicular noise can clearly be heard during parts of the hike. Be sure to bring a generous supply of water, for the morning sun can be quite intense.

To reach the trailhead, drive south from Estes Park on Colorado State Highway 7 for 5.7 miles to the trailhead on the west side of the road. Watch for the sign on the highway designating Lily Mountain. Limited parking is available on both sides of the highway.

The trail begins on a dry, east-facing slope of ponderosa pines. Wide, soft, and easy to walk, the trail traverses the mountain, slowly gaining altitude. Early in the morning, deer tracks may be seen in the sandy soil. In summer you hear the constant clicking of flying grasshoppers.

At 0.8 mile, the path loses a little altitude and comes to a junction. Follow the left fork, which heads up the mountain to the northwest. The right fork continues to descend.

From the fork, the trail climbs steeply up a series of short switchbacks. Large boulders dot the mountainside, providing resting places for weary climbers. Views open to the southeast of Twin Sisters Peaks (11,428 feet), with its green slopes and lumpy rock summit. Enter an area with even larger boulders and good views northeast over Estes Park and Lake Estes. Finally the trail begins to gain altitude seriously amid dense lodgepole pines. Rock cairns mark the way.

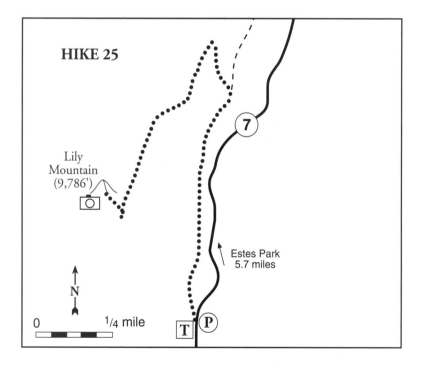

HIKE 25

Lily
Mountain
(9,786')

7

Estes Park
5.7 miles

N

0   1/4 mile

T P

Longs Peak and Mount Meeker from Lily Mountain

The trail suddenly turns to the northwest for the final portion of the ascent. This last section is a scramble over boulders, the direction indicated clearly by cairns. The way is steep, but it is not treacherous.

Once on the summit, Lily Mountain's strategic position becomes apparent. Because the trail ascends the east side of the mountain, the view to the west is hidden until the summit, making the view all the more rewarding. From this lofty perch, the 360-degree view takes in the Mummy Range to the northwest with Mount Chapin (12,454 feet), Mount Chiquita (13,069 feet), and Ypsilon Mountain (13,514 feet); Hallett Peak (12,713 feet) and Flattop Mountain (12,324 feet) to the west; Longs Peak (14,255 feet), Mount Meeker (13,911 feet), and Estes Cone (11,006 feet) to the southwest; Estes Park and Lake Estes to the northeast; and Twin Sisters Peaks to the southeast. Lily Mountain's bare rock summit is a marvelous lunch spot, with a nearly unparalleled view for the altitude gained.

26

Lily Lake

DIFFICULTY: nature stroll, handicapped accessible
    according to uniform federal standards of
    accessibility
DISTANCE: 1-mile loop
USAGE: moderate
STARTING ELEVATION: 8,900 feet; elevation gain, 6 feet
BACKCOUNTRY CAMPSITE: none
SEASON: spring, summer, fall
MAP: USGS 7.5-minute Longs Peak

Constructed in 1997, this delightful, handicapped-accessible trail
takes hikers effortlessly around Lily Lake, providing terrific views
of surrounding peaks, good fishing access, and close encounters
with a lovely variety of wildflowers in spring and summer. At the
lake's west side, a short spur trail, not accessible to wheelchairs,
takes hikers to secluded picnic spots with gorgeous views.

Reach Lily Lake by driving south on Route 7, 6.1 miles from
the intersection of Route 7 and Route 36 in Estes Park. Lily Lake
is located directly across from the Lily Lake Visitor Center on
Route 7. Before strolling around the lake, take a minute to visit
the park's newest visitor center. Inside are numerous interactive
exhibits on park wildlife, weather, history and bird watching.
Rangers are on hand to answer questions, and a good selection
of natural history books are available for sale.

Upon arrival at the shore of Lily Lake, you are greeted with
tremendous views west to Trail Ridge and the Continental Divide.
Begin your hike by walking north, following the lakeside path
counterclockwise. On the lake's north side, pause to appreciate
the impressive views of Longs Peak and Estes Cone across the
lake to the south. The notched summit of Longs Peak (Hike 30)
is easily recognized, for it is the highest peak in the park. Estes
Cone (Hike 28) is the smaller pyramidal peak with the bare rock
summit northeast of Longs Peak. The second-highest peak on the
horizon, just east of Longs Peak, is Mount Meeker.

Anglers will find plenty of access and plenty of company at
Lily Lake. Summer days attract a flotilla of waders and inflatable

craft, as anglers of all ages cast for native cutthroat trout at this spring-fed lake. Despite its name, there are no lily pads to snare lines at Lily Lake, for all of its pond lilies died one winter in the 1930s.

As you make your way up the lake's north side, note the five-needled limber pines that hug the rocky slopes above the lake. Limber pines are excellent rock climbers. Look for their dramatically gnarled shapes near timberline on ledges you'd think would never support a tree. At the lakeshore, keep your eyes peeled for a grand Douglas fir. These magnificent trees are fun for youngsters to identify. Find the large, Christmas tree–shaped conifer whose cones are shaggy with three-pronged bracts. The papery bracts resemble the hind legs and tails of mice jumping for shelter between the scales. No other conifer in the park bears cones quite as interesting.

In summer, a wildflower book is an excellent companion on this hike (a variety are available at the visitor center). Trailside, hikers can readily find yellow blanket flower, wallflower, and golden banner; white cut-leaf daisy, yarrow, and mouse-ear; pink pussy toes, locoweed, and sticky geranium; and pale blue columbine, harebells, and wild flax. There's an especially beautiful field of flax at the west shore of the lake.

Three of these colorful flowers are especially fun to point out to your children. Delicate white mouse-ears are easy to identify because their small white petals come attached in pairs, like tiny mouse ears. Pale pink pussy toes are also true to their name. Their fuzzy, knoblike bracts hide bunches of tiny flowers. Children may like to *gently* touch the furry "toes." A rarer find are the bright pink shooting stars inhabiting the wetter areas of the meadow. These fragrant flowers resemble tiny, dartlike rockets caught in midflight. Native Americans roasted and then ate the roots and leaves of the shooting stars. A good place to find shooting stars is behind the picnic tables, amid the willows, near the end of this hike.

When you've walked to the far west end of the lake (exactly halfway around), look to the right for a wide trail entering from the west. For good views on a half-mile round-trip spur trail, turn right. (This trail is not handicapped accessible.) Almost immediately, turn right again on a wide, rising trail. Walk up the trail for about a quarter mile to a quiet spot affording gorgeous views over a green valley to the impressive peaks of the Mummy Range.

Rock outcrops supply great picnic perches from which to relax and contemplate the scenery. Then retrace your steps back to the Lily Lake Trail and continue your journey around the lake.

The trail continues along the lake's shady south shore. To the north, above the lake, is Lily Mountain (Hike 25), an easy peak for novice climbers. At the southeast edge of the lake, arrive at a marshy area. This is home to the inch-long, striped chorus frog. After a rain, you might be able to hear its call. To initiate a conversation with the frog, take out a pocket comb and run your thumb over the teeth. This sound mimics their call, and you just might get an answer back!

Hikers appreciate Longs Peak and Mount Meeker from Lily Lake

Just before you arrive back at the parking lot, at the south-east edge of the lake, find a small grassy "island." This was an old beaver lodge, now abandoned and grassed over. A few more steps brings you back to the parking area and visitor center.

27

Eugenia Mine

DIFFICULTY: easy
DISTANCE: 1.4 miles one way
USAGE: moderate
STARTING ELEVATION: 9,400 feet; elevation gain,
      508 feet
BACKCOUNTRY CAMPSITE: 1.7 miles from the trailhead
SEASON: summer, fall
MAP: USGS 7.5-minute Longs Peak

This trail leads through pine forest to the ruins of a mine and cabin constructed at the turn of the century. There's not much remaining at the site, so your imagination must fill in what nature has erased. There is, nevertheless, an aura of mystery about the place, and you can send your youngsters searching for clues to the miners' lives amongst the flowers and trees that have grown in the clearing. The site is a good destination for a picnic.

From the junction of US Highway 36 and Colorado State Highway 7 in Estes Park, drive south on Colorado State Highway 7 for 9 miles to a road on the right (west) marked by a sign for the Longs Peak Ranger Station and Campground. Turn right and follow this road for 1 mile, and then turn left for the Longs Peak Ranger Station and parking area. The trailhead is next to the ranger station.

Begin on the Longs Peak Trail, which gains nearly 5,000 feet in its 8-mile climb to the summit of Longs Peak. From the start, the trail steadily but gently gains altitude. After 0.5 mile, the trail to Eugenia Mine enters from the right (north). Take the right fork, which arrives at the mine in 0.9 mile.

Inn Brook near Eugenia Mine and cabin ruins

The wide trail rolls gently through a forest of predominantly lodgepole pine. In the summer the trail is dry and often warm because the tall, straight pines provide little shade. Watch for some old conifers of tremendous girth and unusual configuration to break the monotony. The trail is well used by horses, whose calling card is frequently encountered.

Watch for squirrel middens along the trail, places where red squirrels cache their pine cones. Occasionally successive generations of squirrels use the same burial place, resulting in enormous middens that can be as long as 20 feet. Evidence of a midden appears as a pile of pine-cone cores and scales, sometimes in a hollow log or stump. Pine-cone cores look like the remains of a miniature corn cob, for squirrels remove the seeds of a pine cone just as people eat corn on the cob.

The mining site, located immediately after Inn Brook, is a good place to picnic. The shallow brook is perfect for children to explore, and the cool water is a welcome relief for hot toes. Along the water's edge, wildflowers flourish. The actual mine and tailing piles are a few hundred feet upstream and west (left) of the cabin. Climb steeply up the slope above the tailings to find several more digging sites.

The once sturdy cabin whose walls now barely stand was the property of Carl P. Norwall and his family, who lived at the site and worked the unproductive mine in the early 1900s. The Norwalls had two daughters and a very comfortable, well-furnished home, which included a piano. Reportedly, the piano and the Norwall daughters attracted many young miners and travelers from miles away. Despite the relative elegance by which

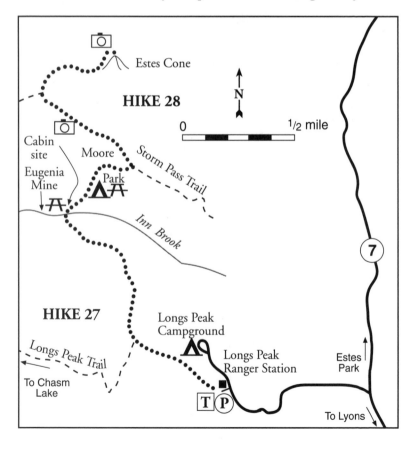

the Norwalls lived in this pleasant forest clearing, the mine proved unsuccessful. The mine was dug more than 1,000 feet into Battle Mountain but delivered no valuable lode. The last filing claim for the mine occurred in 1919. The Norwalls seem to have abandoned the site shortly thereafter.

Children enjoy "discovering" the mine tailings and old cabin and searching for scattered pieces of machinery. One curious piece of machinery hidden amid the trees resembles the Tin Woodsman in *The Wizard of Oz.* Even the setting is right. To a child, it might also look like an ancient space capsule. These types of ruins are not spectacular, but they are fun.

Be careful to leave the site exactly as found. Do not harm, alter, or remove any objects from the site. Children should not climb on the remains, which may be fragile. Finally, never let children enter an abandoned mine.

HIKING OPTIONS:

(1) The trail to the right of the cabin heads northeast 0.4 mile to Moore Park, a small, well-flowered meadow. This short and easy trip is highly recommended. Backpackers will find a nice campsite at Moore Park. (2) The same trail reaches Estes Cone (Hike 28) in 1.9 miles—a strenuous but rewarding climb.

28

Estes Cone

DIFFICULTY: strenuous
DISTANCE: 3.3 miles one way
USAGE: moderate
STARTING ELEVATION: 9,400 feet; elevation gain,
        1,606 feet
BACKCOUNTRY CAMPSITE: 1.7 miles from the trailhead
SEASON: summer, fall
MAP: USGS 7.5-minute Longs Peak

The climb to the summit of Estes Cone through steep forested slopes is not long, but it is very demanding. The summit is extremely satisfying, however, and has exceptional views. Along the way, visit the ruins of Eugenia Mine and the well-flowered meadow of Moore Park.

Drive to the Longs Peak Trailhead and hike to Eugenia Mine, as described in Hike 27. From the mine, the trail heads northeast, gently descending after 0.4 mile to Moore Park. This small meadow is a jewel in midsummer, sporting an abundance of multicolored wildflowers. The campsite at Moore Park would make an excellent destination for young backpackers because it lies only 1.7 miles from the trailhead, and the trail to it gains only 354 feet in elevation.

The trail leads through Moore Park, arriving in 0.1 mile at a junction with the Storm Pass Trail. Turn left (uphill). The trail rises up a sunny south-facing slope covered with lodgepole pines. The break in the trees on the left provides a good view of Mount Meeker and Longs Peak. As the trail steepens, limber pines and wildflowers appear. Look for red Indian paintbrush and purple composites.

After 0.6 mile, come to the trail leading to the summit and turn right. The trail switchbacks very steeply up the slope. When the trail disappears, watch for cairns to show the way.

Estes Cone

The last portion of the hike requires scrambling over large boulders. Though not particularly dangerous, this stretch is tiring and requires care, especially with young climbers. Very near the top, reach a false summit. Then descend slightly and rise over the last boulders to the peak.

The view from the summit is magnificent in all directions. To the east, you can see Twin Sisters Peaks (11,428 feet); to the northeast, Lily Mountain (9,786 feet) (Hike 25); to the north, Lake Estes; to the northwest, Ypsilon Mountain (13,514 feet) and the Mummy Range (Hike 24); to the west, Hallett Peak (12,713 feet) (Hike 17); to the southwest, Battle Mountain (12,044 feet); and to the south, Mount Meeker (13,911 feet) and Longs Peak (14,255 feet) (Hike 30).

Estes Cone can be seen prominently on the west side of Colorado State Highway 7, as well as from various places in the park, including Trail Ridge Road. The peak stands out in the landscape because it is so perfectly cone-shaped. After this difficult climb, look with pride at the rocky summit, which, for one afternoon, was all yours.

29

Chasm Lake

DIFFICULTY: strenuous
DISTANCE: 4.2 miles one way
USAGE: high
STARTING ELEVATION: 9,400 feet; elevation gain,
      2,360 feet
BACKCOUNTRY CAMPSITE: 1.2 miles from the trailhead
SEASON: summer, fall
MAP: USGS 7.5-minute Longs Peak

This strenuous hike rises through thick forest to alpine tundra and climbs to a large lake dramatically set at the base of the park's tallest peak. The trail to Chasm Lake is one of the finest in the park. Scenic views, abundant wildflowers, and the exceptional beauty of the lake make it one of the park's most popular. To enjoy Chasm Lake to the fullest, start your hike as early as possible. And don't forget your binoculars.

Drive to the Longs Peak Trailhead, as described in Hike 27, and climb the Longs Peak Trail to the junction with the path to Eugenia Mine and Moore Park. Do not turn right; continue straight ahead, climbing amid firs and spruce. At approximately 1 mile, reach Alpine Brook, a cool and welcome rest stop. The trail continues to climb, following the brook. At 1.2 miles from the trailhead, arrive at the Goblins Camp backcountry campsite. If your young campers can carry their packs 1.2 miles and up 820 feet, this is a fine place to camp. The stand of strangely gnarled limber pines probably gave the campsite its name.

After numerous short switchbacks, cross a bridge over Alpine Brook and enter a riot of colorful flowers. A fine view momentarily opens up to the east, revealing the lumpy summit of Twin Sisters Peaks (11,428 feet).

As you climb, the trees get visibly shorter until, at timberline, you pass the last trees able to survive the severe temperatures, short growing season, and howling winds at 10,700 feet. Winds of over 200 miles per hour have been measured on Longs Peak in the winter. The strong winds create "banner trees," which have limbs only on their protected (leeward) side.

Switchback up Mills Moraine to a trail junction, about 3 miles from the trailhead. Climbers head to the right for the Boulder Field and the summit of Longs Peak. The left fork takes you to Chasm Lake. There is a toilet near the junction.

To the right at the junction is Jims Grove, which is currently closed for restoration. This area of picturesque limber pines is named for the infamous Estes Park mountain man, Jim Nugent. One of the most colorful characters in the history of this area, Jim lived in Estes Park from the 1860s until his murder in 1874. He was reputed to be a handsome man but only in profile, for a grizzly bear had severely mauled one side of his face. In 1873, Jim accompanied one of the first women to climb Longs Peak. Isabella Bird's fascinating account of the climb and of her travels in the area is memorialized in *A Lady's Life in the Rocky Mountains*.

In the morning the view to the east over the foothills reveals waves of purple resembling the shadowy mountains of a Japanese woodcut. To the west, the massive east face of Longs Peak inspires the mountain climber in everyone.

Follow cairns up Mills Moraine. The trail leads to the edge of the gorge of the Roaring Fork River, where there are views of Peacock Pool below, Columbine Falls spilling over the top of the gorge, and the face of Longs Peak towering above. The trail leading to the falls descends slightly. Walk carefully on the narrow ridge and, if snow remains on this narrow path, proceed with extreme caution.

From Columbine Falls, white rivulets fall over 100 feet to the dark pond of Peacock Pool, which resembles the intense blue "eye" of a peacock feather. Yellow cinquefoil profusely grace the mountainside. The real treat is the abundance of Colorado blue columbine near the head of the falls. With its intense blue sepals and white petals, the Colorado blue columbine is unmistakable.

Above the falls, walk through a lushly flowered meadow beside sparkling Roaring Fork. The intimacy of this wild garden forms a pleasing contrast to the sheer cliffs that loom overhead. Be careful not to stray from the path, for this beautiful meadow is just recovering from overuse.

The trail heads toward the Park Service rescue cabin at the end of the meadow. Travel past the cabin, following cairns marking the easiest route up a ledge. Youngsters might need assistance on this short but tricky ascent.

Chasm Lake is not visible until the top of the ledge is reached. This large tarn was carved by a glacier that flowed down from Longs Peak. When the ice pulled away from the peak, it took part of the mountain with it. The resulting cliffs form a dramatic amphitheater. The sheer east face of Longs Peak, the "Diamond,"

The east face of Longs Peak from Chasm Lake

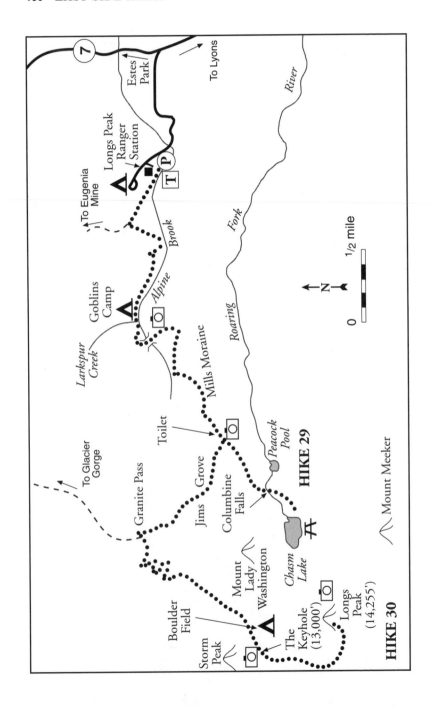

rises 2,500 feet above the lake. The Diamond is a favorite playground for steel-nerved rock climbers. With binoculars, you can watch their rare and terrifying ballet.

The lake is a wonderful place for a well-deserved picnic. Marmots, who den in the rocky slopes, are certain to greet you. Watch also for the smaller and livelier pikas, which can be seen scurrying back and forth over the tundra rocks. Please do not feed the wildlife.

30

Longs Peak

DIFFICULTY: very strenuous
DISTANCE: 8 miles one way
USAGE: high
STARTING ELEVATION: 9,400 feet; elevation gain
      4,855 feet
BACKCOUNTRY CAMPSITE: 1.2, 2.8 (group site), and
      6 miles from the trailhead
SEASON: summer
MAP: USGS 7.5-minute Longs Peak

Climbing Longs Peak is a thrilling, once-in-a-lifetime experience. It is also arduous, exhausting, sometimes scary, and potentially dangerous. The highest mountain in the park and the fifteenth highest in the state, Longs Peak is a magnificent mountain whose distinctive summit inspires dreams long after you leave its shadow. Though immensely difficult, the climb is also beautiful and diverse, continuously challenging the hiker with varying terrains. If weather, nerves, or weariness frustrates the climb, the hike to any of a number of milestones is still fun and worthwhile. All summit climbers should be comfortable with boulder-hopping, scrambling, steep drop-offs, and passage along narrow ledges.

Please heed the following precautions with the utmost seriousness. Over 35 people have died climbing Longs Peak since 1884. Your level of preparedness will help prevent serious accidents.

- Start early. Because of the high risk of lightning strikes above treeline, you need to leave the summit by noon, at the latest. Even if the sky looks clear, abide by this time restriction. Storms develop very suddenly and without warning. Adult climbers should allow 7 to 8 hours for the ascent and 5 hours for the descent. Families must begin before the sun rises. Depending on the speed of your group, start between 2 and 4 A.M.
- Bring a minimum of 1 quart of liquid per person. Two quarts is better. All water sources on the mountain must be treated before drinking.
- Prepare for stormy weather by carrying warm clothes and rain gear.
- Watch for symptoms of altitude sickness, and descend immediately if symptoms appear. Make sure all members of your group are acclimatized to high altitude before climbing.
- Protect your skin by wearing a hat, sunscreen, and lip cream.
- Do not push an exhausted climber of any age to reach the summit. Most accidents happen on the descent. Resist the urge to be overly goal-oriented. Make this a fun, safe climb.
- The ascent may be made in 2 days by camping at one of the designated backcountry sites, but permits must be obtained beforehand. Reservations are often made months in advance for these popular sites.
- Check snow conditions on the peak with a ranger at the Longs Peak Ranger Station. From October to June, snow usually remains on the summit, making this a *technical* climb, requiring rope, crampons, ice axes, and technical expertise.
- Above all, turn back when common sense dictates, whether because of illness, weakness, injury, vertigo, time, or the weather. There is always another day!

To climb Longs Peak, follow the trail description for Hike 29 to the intersection atop Mills Moraine about 3 miles from the trailhead. At the junction, head right for the Boulder Field and Longs Peak. Most likely, Longs Peak climbers will be hiking in the pre-dawn darkness to this point. Bring flashlights, watch your footing, and rejoice in the knowledge that the trail will look new on the way down.

Cross Alpine Brook and enter a wind-sculpted forest of limber pine called Jims Grove. Climb, rising gently below the east face of Mount Lady Washington. About 0.7 mile from the trail junction at Mills Moraine, reach Granite Pass and the intersection with the North Longs Peak Trail. Granite Pass is a significant achievement. You've ascended above 12,000 feet and already climbed over 2,600 feet. (That's over half the vertical feet of the total climb.) Most hikers are likely to feel the thinness of the air at this altitude. Slow your pace, drink plenty of fluids, and apply ample sunscreen.

At the Granite Pass junction, head left (west) and ascend via demanding switchbacks. After the switchbacks, the grade moderates. From Granite Pass, it's about 2 miles to the Boulder Field, an immense moonscape of large rocks tucked dramatically below the sheer north face of Longs. Nine unique backcountry campsites lie amid the boulders, hidden within circular stone walls. From these sites, moonlit views of the mountains are exceptional.

From the Boulder Field, it is only 2 miles to the summit, but it's a tough couple of miles. Pin your sights first on the Keyhole, an oval notch in the ridge between Longs and Storm Peaks, about 0.5 mile beyond the Boulder Field and a steep climb of about 500 feet. Shortly before the Keyhole, catch your breath at a stone hut, built in memory of two climbers who perished during a winter ascent in 1925.

Reaching the Keyhole (13,000 feet) is only second-best to reaching the summit. Looking beyond the Keyhole to the west, an incredible panorama of magnificent peaks, valleys, lakes, and streams comes into view. Before you spreads an unparalleled view of Glacier Gorge, where three peaks over 13,000 feet form an amphitheater opening to the north. This view alone is well worth the climb.

Check your watch. From the Keyhole, the summit is 1.5 miles away with an elevation gain of about 1,200 feet, a hike of at least 2 hours. If the sky looks stormy already (especially to the west), turn back.

Past the Keyhole, follow red and yellow bull's-eyes. Descend first along an exposed ledge traversing under the west face of Longs. After about 0.3 mile on the ledge, reach the Trough, a long gully filled with loose stones. Ascend the steep gully, taking care not to kick loose rocks that might injure climbers below. Snow often remains in the Trough long into the summer.

After a tiring half-mile climb, reach the Narrows, a ledge that exposes climbers to a steep drop-off. The ledge is wide enough for most (it is not steep and approaches sidewalk width in places), but it does narrow to a couple of feet in one section. Many will find this passage a bit terrifying. After several hundred feet of the Narrows, arrive at the Homestretch, wide slabs of granite lying at a steep incline all the way to the summit. Climbers must make their way up the smooth granite, about 450 vertical feet, to reach Longs' flat summit. The safest way is to use both hands and stay low to the rock, as the angle of incline is very steep.

Finally, arrive at the summit. For posterity, climbers will want to sign the summit register. Then relax and refresh yourself on the multi-acre summit. There are unforgettable views in *all* directions. You have earned the most awe-inspiring view in Rocky Mountain National Park.

Time and weather will pull you from the summit. To safely descend the Homestretch, try a slow fanny descent. Take extra care to reach the Keyhole safely. Descending these steep sections, especially the Trough, can be tricky, especially if you're fatigued.

It is important to keep the group moving to reach treeline before storms move in. Thus weary hikers must push on past the Boulder Field and Granite Pass. Upon descending past Jims Grove, you can relax and congratulate yourself on a climb to remember for a lifetime.

31

Copeland Falls

DIFFICULTY: nature stroll, handicapped access with
     assistance
DISTANCE: 0.3 mile one way
USAGE: high
STARTING ELEVATION: 8,500 feet; elevation gain, 15 feet
BACKCOUNTRY CAMPSITE: none
SEASON: spring, summer, fall
MAP: USGS 7.5-minute Allens Park

This is a delightful hike on a wide path through a well-flowered subalpine forest to a small waterfall. A great variety of trees, flowers, birds, and small mammals grace the area. In the fall, Rocky

Hiking to Copeland Falls

Mountain maples and quaking aspens light up the trail with red and yellow.

Drive 12.7 miles south from Estes Park on Colorado State Highway 7 to a signed road on the right (west) leading to the Wild Basin Ranger Station. Turn right on this road and take the first right fork after Wild Basin Lodge onto a narrow, unpaved road marked with signs for the ranger station and Copeland Lake. Follow the unpaved road for 2 miles to a parking lot at the Wild Basin Ranger Station. The trailhead is located at the south end of the lot.

The hike begins by crossing Hunters Creek on a wooden bridge. Flowers dot the forest floor with color, and aspens tremble in the breeze. The vanillalike fragrance of the mature ponderosa pines fills the air. The variety of trees, flowering shrubs, and wildflowers creates a lovely, gentle, and immensely inviting setting.

Among the wildflowers, watch for the deep yellow wallflower, whose four-petaled flowers are arranged on its stem like miniature bouquets. The wallflower got its name by its tendency to grow beside walls. Unpopular girls at dances were called wallflowers because they also had a tendency to line the dance-hall walls. Native Americans and settlers used the seeds of this member of the mustard family as a flavoring.

The abundant flowering shrub beside the trail is wild rose, which sports pink five-petaled blossoms from late May to mid-July. Red rose hips, a fruit savored by many varieties of wildlife, including black bear, replace the flowers in late summer. Native Americans found many medicinal uses for wild rose, including applying the stem, in powdered form, to wounds as a way of reducing scarring. The Indians also blew ground rose petals into sore throats.

The trail is level to Copeland Falls, but may be wet in several places. Puddles are easily dodged by hikers, but a wheelchair or stroller will need assistance.

After 0.3 mile, small Copeland Falls appears. The waterfall is pleasant but unspectacular. Nevertheless, the clearing by the falls makes an excellent picnic spot if the summer crowds have not yet arrived. If the falls are crowded, stroll a short distance up the trail to find a quiet place along the North St. Vrain Creek, where a wealth of gentle riverbank awaits exploration.

HIKING OPTIONS:

(1) Continue 1.5 miles and climb 685 feet to Calypso Cascades (see Hike 32). (2) Continue 2.4 miles and climb 935 feet to Ouzel Falls (see Hike 33).

32

Calypso Cascades

DIFFICULTY: easy
DISTANCE: 1.8 miles one way
USAGE: high
STARTING ELEVATION: 8,500 feet; elevation gain,
      700 feet
BACKCOUNTRY CAMPSITE: 1.4 miles from the trailhead
SEASON: spring, summer, fall
MAP: USGS 7.5-minute Allens Park

This short, scenic hike leads past Copeland Falls through lovely subalpine forest to roaring Calypso Cascades. Wildflowers, a

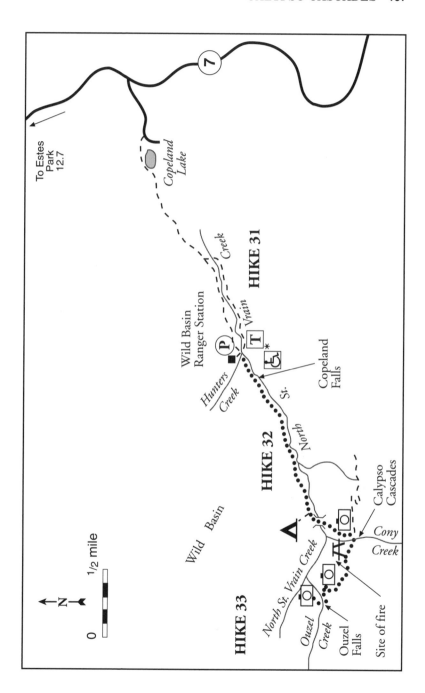

multitude of birds, and the North St. Vrain Creek accompany the hiker. Walk just a little beyond Calypso Cascades to see the site of the 1978 Wild Basin fire, where fireweed blooms radiant pink against a mountainside of blackened trunks. Start early to avoid summer crowds and to secure a parking place at the trailhead.

As described in Hike 31, drive to the Wild Basin Ranger Station and hike to Copeland Falls. Continue past the falls. The trail becomes sunnier and drier, and to the left are many spur trails leading to the North St. Vrain Creek, a couple of yards away.

Rocky Mountain maple appears by the trail, adding brilliant red color in the fall. Look also for the conical stumps of aspens that have been cut by beaver. At one time this area was rich with this industrious and luxuriously furred rodent. The North St. Vrain Creek was named, in fact, for a nineteenth-century trading post located on this creek, where Indians and mountain men brought their beaver pelts.

Farther down the trail, enter a dense forest of lodgepole pines. Within this forest, just before a substantial wood bridge across the creek, a trail to the right leads to Pine Ridge backcountry campsite. Located only 1.4 miles from and 400 feet higher than the trailhead, this campsite would be a good destination for young backpackers.

At 1.4 miles from the trailhead you reach the bridge across the North St. Vrain Creek, which offers a nice view of the rushing water below. Take a moment to watch this spectacle before beginning the ascent to Calypso Cascades. After the bridge, the serious climb to the falls begins. The well-constructed trail gains 300 feet quickly, leaving North St. Vrain Creek to follow Cony Creek due south. Stairs help you rise rapidly above Cony Creek. Just before Calypso Cascades there is a large flat boulder upon which to stand for good views over Wild Basin and to the mountains beyond. Soon after, the trail levels and arrives at the cascades.

You are well rewarded for your climb. Water rushes madly over the rocks. The water-chilled air rising from the cascade provides welcome coolness after the climb. In the falls, tree trunks washed bare by the water crisscross the rocks. Just beyond Calypso Cascades are large boulders for picnicking.

Through the month of June, search the ground near the falls in moist shady spots for the Calypso orchid, also known as the fairy slipper. Large patches of this delicate pink flower once blanketed the area. Greedy admirers, however, left few for today's hikers. Be sure you do not crush or pick these beauties; leave them to delight and multiply.

For a worthwhile side trip, walk the trail a short distance west, beyond the falls, to the area burned by the Ouzel Lake fire of August 9, 1978. This area features wildflowers, a graveyard of charred stumps, and good views to the north and east. For more information on this fire, see Hike 33.

HIKING OPTIONS:

To visit beautiful Ouzel Falls from Calypso Cascades, continue on the trail to the west for 0.9 mile and an elevation gain of 250 feet (see Hike 33).

Testing the water near Calypso Cascades

33

Ouzel Falls

DIFFICULTY: moderate
DISTANCE: 2.7 miles one way
USAGE: high
STARTING ELEVATION: 8,500 feet; elevation gain,
    950 feet
BACKCOUNTRY CAMPSITE: 1.4 miles from the trailhead
SEASON: summer, fall
MAP: USGS 7.5-minute Allens Park

This wonderful hike offers great diversity: two fine waterfalls, a lovely trail through subalpine forest, and a traverse through an area badly burned by a fire, but with fine views and marvelous wildflowers. For a measure of solitude, hike in the early morning, before the crowds arrive at the trailhead.

Drive to the Wild Basin Trailhead, as described in Hike 31, and hike 1.8 miles to Calypso Cascades, as described in Hike 32. At the Cascades, take the trail to the right, heading west. The trail crosses Cony Creek on two bridges, then leaves the creek to traverse an east-facing slope and enters the area burned by the 1978 fire. Started by lightning at Ouzel Lake, approximately 3 miles away, the fire was the largest in the history of the park, burning 1,050 acres. Ten years later, this fire would seem small in comparison to the Yellowstone fire, which burned more than 1,000 times as much acreage.

Naturally occurring fires play an important and generally beneficial role in the park. Small, relatively frequent fires create new meadows and shrublands in a patchwork pattern, thereby providing a rich variety of habitats for plants and wildlife. In this way, fires increase the diversity and populations of flora and fauna. Naturalists know that fire suppression is detrimental. Where natural fires are not allowed, great stores of downed timber and other forest fuels build to dangerous levels. Fire suppression in Yellowstone from 1880 to 1970 contributed to the severity of the 1989 fires, which were fed by 90 years' worth of kindling.

Hiking across this charred mountainside, marvel at the power of fire and the changes it brings. Blackened stumps extend for acres. The area is brightened by the superior views of Longs Peak and Mount Meeker to the northeast and by the bright colors of flowers that have taken over what was once dark forest. Note especially the bright pink fireweed that covers the area. This plant is one of the first to appear after fire strips the land.

Fire created a new feeding area for deer and elk on the open hillside. Watch for them among the fireweed. Admire, too, the innumerable butterflies. Hopping from flower to flower, butterflies sample each blossom through taste organs in their feet. An initial taste determines whether they will insert their long, coiled tongues to sip the nectar.

One activity for the children is to use a small piece of charred wood to make charcoal drawings. Bring a sketch pad and let them draw or make rubbings. Please do not carry out the charcoal; removing natural objects from the park is against regulations.

After 0.4 mile, the trail begins to switchback up to the falls, accompanied by the sound of the rushing waterfall. Continue to climb the rocky slope, following the water music. Ouzel Falls, a magnificent chute of water, plunging a good distance to Ouzel Creek, can best be seen by carefully climbing up the slope on the south side of the falls, just before the bridge over Ouzel Creek. The rocks can be slippery, so children should be closely supervised.

Ouzel Falls was named for the highly entertaining water ouzel, or dipper. Look for this chunky brown bird, which resembles a wren, diving in the rushing water in search of small fish and insects. The superbly adapted dipper is able to walk on the bottom of streams, swim underwater, and fly behind waterfalls. The bird builds its nest on rocky ledges, often within the spray of a waterfall, where its eggs are safe from predators.

Before returning to the trailhead, indulge in a short detour for a marvelous view. Continue up the trail after Ouzel Falls, crossing the bridge over Ouzel Creek. About 100 yards past the bridge is a rocky overlook, offering superb views of Wild Basin, Mount Meeker, and Longs Peak.

CHAPTER
3

Trail Ridge Hikes

The trails in this section all lead above treeline, offering magnificent views of surrounding mountains and intimate encounters with the strange and beautiful tundra. These hikes are spectacular and rewarding, but extra precautions must be taken when hiking in the high country. Observe the following guidelines to protect both yourself and the fragile tundra.

For Your Protection
- Begin hiking early so that you can be off the trail by early afternoon, when summer thunderstorms begin.

  The tundra is a dangerous place during a storm because lightning seeks the tallest object in a landscape, which, unfortunately, may be you.
- Bring warm clothes, including hats and gloves.

  The average summer temperature is only 50 degrees, and the ever-present wind (averaging 25 miles per hour in the summer) makes wind chill a significant factor.
- Apply sunscreen liberally.

  The risk of sunburn is greater at high altitudes due to increased ultraviolet radiation.
- Acclimate your group to the park's altitude before trying a long Trail Ridge hike.

  You'll enjoy the hike more if your body has had a chance to adjust to the thin air.
- Be alert to signs of altitude sickness, including nausea, headaches, dizziness, and shortness of breath.

If someone in your group feels uncomfortable, return to a lower altitude at once. Pressing onward would be a serious mistake, especially if children are affected.
- Take it easy; hiking in the high country is more demanding and requires a measured pace.

For the Protection of the Tundra
- Minimize the impact of off-trail hiking by stepping on rocks whenever possible and by avoiding single-file hiking.

   Never leave the trail in areas where signs indicate that off-trail travel is prohibited. Such areas include Forest Canyon Overlook (Hike 36), Rock Cut (Hike 38), and Fall River Pass Tundra Trail (Hike 40). When in doubt about the permissibility of off-trail hiking, ask a park ranger.
- Never pick tundra flowers; a plant the size of a quarter may be centuries old.
- Carry out all refuse, even organic matter.

   On the tundra, it can take years for an orange peel to decompose. Furthermore, litter blocks the precious light needed by underlying tundra plants. One naturalist noted that a beer can left behind on the tundra destroys 50 to 100 years' worth of plant growth and lasts for at least a century.
- Never enter areas closed for revegetation; it may take 100 years for trampled tundra to repair itself.

———————————————— **34** ————————————————

Indian Game Drive System Trail

DIFFICULTY: easy
DISTANCE: 0.75 mile one way
USAGE: low
STARTING ELEVATION: 11,280 feet; elevation gain,
   160 feet
BACKCOUNTRY CAMPSITE: none
SEASON: summer, early fall
MAP: USGS 7.5-minute Trail Ridge

Search for ancient Indian ruins, enter trailless wilderness, spot deer and elk, and enjoy nearly limitless vistas on this excellent

Trail Ridge Road

hike for older children. For a short hike, head straight to what may be an Indian game drive system (6,000-year-old stone walls used for hunting by prehistoric people), or spend hours exploring the surrounding tundra. Because there is no trail to the ruins, a compass and USGS topographic map are necessary—and be sure you know how to use them.

A bit of ancient history will enhance this unusual hike. Archaeologists suspect that the first human presence in Rocky Mountain National Park occurred 10,000 to 15,000 years ago. The finding of crafted stone Clovis projectile points on Trail Ridge suggests that prehistoric peoples occasionally may have used Trail Ridge as an east-west route.

Approximately 8,000 years ago, humans began to appear more regularly in these mountains. Numerous projectile points found in the park from this period indicate that seasonal hunting attracted Indians to the mountains and valleys. These ancient people may have constructed game drive systems high on Trail Ridge.

An Indian game drive system is a V-shaped series of low rock walls constructed to funnel game such as elk, sheep, bison, and deer to dugouts at the end of the walls, where Indians laid in wait. Such systems were necessary because natural cover was scarce. More than 40 Indian game drive systems have been found along the Front Range.

Some archaeologists believe that the rock formations seen on this hike are remnants of an Indian game drive system. The pattern of stones is similar to other game drive systems found in the Rockies. Although some experts question the authenticity of the formation, the hike to the purported relics is still fascinating.

To reach the trailhead, park at a small turnout on Trail Ridge Road, 1.5 miles west of Rainbow Curve. The parking area is the first pullout on the left after Rainbow Curve. For eastbound travelers on Trail Ridge Road, the parking area is the second pullout on the right, 1.4 miles east of Forest Canyon Overlook. To reach Trail Ridge Road from the east, begin at the Beaver Meadows Entrance Station and drive 2.9 miles northwest on US Highway 36 to Deer Ridge Junction. Continue straight ahead on US Highway 34, which at this point becomes Trail Ridge Road. To reach Trail Ridge Road from the west, begin at the Grand Lake Entrance Station and drive north on US Highway 34, which becomes Trail Ridge Road at Milner Pass.

The hike begins at a break in the trees on the thickly covered slope above the turnout. Climb the slope through thick elfinwood on a faint path heading south and over a small rise, emerging from the elfinwood in a level area dotted with islands of *krummholz*. To the right (west) is Tombstone Ridge. Head away from the ridge and around the tree islands in a southeasterly direction.

After hiking through the area of tree islands, arrive at the top of the treeless slope that heads down to Trail Ridge Road. Look carefully on the mountainside below. You should see several low rock "walls," badly eroded, in V-shaped configurations, aiming down the mountainside. Climb down for closer examination, but take your time on the steep slope. From the ridge above the slope, enjoy excellent views of the Mummy Range to the north and of Horseshoe Park below.

An early start on this hike brings rich rewards. The *krummholz* woods are a popular habitat for deer and elk in the summer, offering succulent grazing and protection from the wind. Numerous other animals also enjoy the shelter of the *krummholz's* scraggly branches, including snowshoe hares.

Ptarmigan in summer plumage

HIKING OPTIONS:

Just west of Tombstone Ridge is the Upper Old Ute Trail (Hike 35). To reach this trail from the Indian game drive system, hike west through a break in Tombstone Ridge. The Upper Old Ute Trail is clearly visible on the other side of Tombstone Ridge.

35

Upper Old Ute Trail

DIFFICULTY: moderate
DISTANCE: 2 miles one way
USAGE: moderate
STARTING ELEVATION: 11,440 feet; elevation gain,
      160 feet
BACKCOUNTRY CAMPSITE: none
SEASON: summer, early fall
MAP: USGS 7.5-minute Trail Ridge

This beautiful tundra trail offers superior views, alpine wildflowers, and Indian history. The easy, mostly level hike leaves you with plenty of energy for exploring its many attractions, including off-trail rock scrambling for older youngsters and plenty of

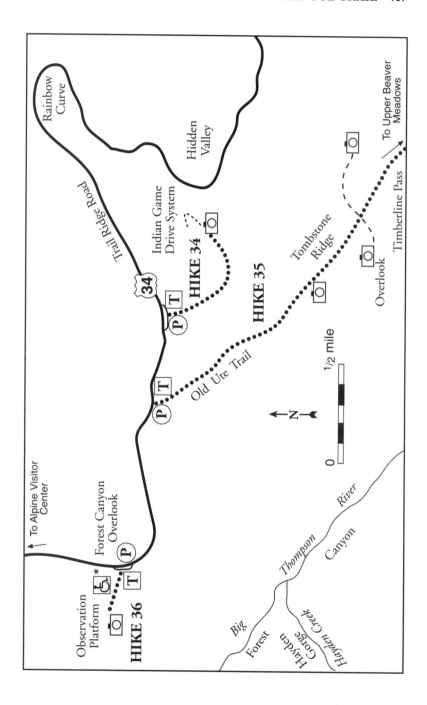

wildlife for younger siblings. At dawn or dusk on sunny summer days, deer, elk, and marmots are plentiful. The trail offers the same spectacular scenery as the popular Rock Cut, Fall River Pass, and Forest Canyon Overlook trails, without the pavement, crowds, and noise.

The Old Ute Trail Trailhead is located on the south side of Trail Ridge Road (US Highway 34), 13 miles from the Beaver Meadows Entrance Station (2 miles west of Rainbow Curve) and 7 miles east of the Alpine Visitor Center (0.8 mile east of Forest Canyon Overlook). Parking is limited at the trailhead; a few more spaces are located a short distance up the road, to the east. The trailhead is marked by a small sign.

Archaeologists believe that prehistoric peoples used the Old Ute Trail for seasonal east-west passage across the Front Range at least 6,000 years ago and perhaps as early as 15,000 years ago. Clovis stone projectile points used by Paleo-Indians 10,000 to 15,000 years ago have been found along Trail Ridge. However, it is possible that later Indians might have brought these ancient projectile points to Trail Ridge.

Native Americans regularly used the Old Ute Trail. Although there is no evidence that Indian tribes lived inside what is now Rocky Mountain National Park, the Ute and Arapaho peoples used its meadows for hunting and gathering and traveled across

Longs Peak from Old Ute Trail (Photo by Ned Strong)

its mountain passes. The Utes resided mainly on the west side of the Rockies, the Arapaho on the east. Both used the rich hunting grounds of the Great Plains and the park's mountain habitats. The common use of hunting grounds led to hostilities and frequent raids across the mountains in the 1800s. One historian recounted the Arapaho belief that the "Man Above created the Rockies as a barrier to separate them and the . . . Utes." Memorable tales of tribal life and battles may be heard at evening campfire programs at the park. Evidence of the Indians' use of this area in the form of arrowheads and stone campfire rings are occasionally still found by fortunate and observant hikers.

The trail begins by climbing a low rise at a very gentle grade. Rock cairns mark the way. To the right is a good view into Forest Canyon; look across the canyon to the high peaks of the Continental Divide.

As the trail rounds a bend, Trail Ridge Road disappears from view. Here, out of sight of the highway, you can imagine what the Utes and Arapaho saw as they crossed over roadless and wild mountains.

To the south, Longs Peak's boxy summit is approximately 10 miles away and almost 3,000 feet above you, but on a clear day it looks well within reach. At this altitude, distances are deceiving. The clarity of the air makes far objects appear closer than they might at lower elevations. This illusion can frustrate hikers for whom a distant peak appears tantalizingly close.

After a quarter mile, the trail heads toward ominous-looking Tombstone Ridge. Look for yellow-bellied marmots sunning themselves on the rocks to the right of the trail. Midmorning and midafternoon are excellent times to watch these chubby relatives of the woodchuck. When startled, they sometimes issue a sharp whistle of alarm (marmots have been called "whistle pigs"). A softer, higher pitched whistle is likely to be the call of the elusive pika, a small, round-eared relative of the rabbit. Called the farmer of the tundra, the little gray pika will most likely be scurrying about gathering flowers and grasses for its winter stockpile.

Early in the morning, waves of purple peaks define the horizon to the east. Early morning hikers may also catch glimpses of deer and elk grazing on the tundra. Watch for them to the east, after a break in the ridge.

Exploring the ridges is a rewarding and adventurous activity. From atop Tombstone Ridge, enjoy an excellent view of the

Mummy Range to the north and winding Trail Ridge Road far below. Do not let children climb unsupervised, however, for the rocks can be slippery and unstable.

Where the trail begins to descend to Windy Gulch, another interesting climb heads off-trail to the right. Head for the rock outcropping just above treeline. This formation looks purposefully constructed, as if Indians had built it to serve as a lookout for game or approaching tribes. The lookout offers splendid views over Forest Canyon to Fern Lake, with Flattop Mountain and Hallett Peak rising dramatically above the lake. Estes Park is visible to the east, Mount Richthofen and the Never Summer Range to the west. Again, the rocks can be slippery and unstable.

The lookout marks a good place to turn around. From here, the trail descends to treeline and makes its way to Upper Beaver Meadows, 4.5 miles away, losing almost 3,000 feet in elevation from the trailhead.

HIKING OPTIONS:

(1) If two cars are available, you can hike a long section of the Old Ute Trail (6.5 downhill miles), from Trail Ridge to Upper Beaver Meadows. (2) The Upper Old Ute Trail can also be easily combined with Hike 34, the Indian Game Drive System Trail.

36

Forest Canyon Overlook

DIFFICULTY: nature stroll, handicapped access with
    assistance
DISTANCE: 0.25 mile one way
USAGE: high
STARTING ELEVATION: 11,720 feet; elevation loss,
    100 feet
BACKCOUNTRY CAMPSITE: none
SEASON: summer, early fall
MAP: USGS 7.5-minute Trail Ridge

Abundant wildflowers, small mammals, fabulous views, and a blast of cold alpine air all await you at Forest Canyon Overlook.

Terra Tomah Mountain

A short paved path crosses flowery tundra to an observation platform over vast Forest Canyon. From the overlook, admire the work of glaciers, which carved mountain spires and lake-filled cirques. Across the canyon of the Big Thompson River, 2,500 feet below, are the rugged peaks of the Continental Divide. On the rocks below the observation platform, look for marmots and pikas.

To reach Forest Canyon Overlook from the Beaver Meadows Entrance Station, drive 2.9 miles west on US Highway 36 to Deer Ridge Junction. Take the left fork and drive US Highway 34— Trail Ridge Road—for 11.1 miles. Forest Canyon Overlook is on the left (west) side of the highway. There is a large parking lot at the overlook.

Although the views from the overlook are truly magnificent, the spot can be desperately overcrowded in the summer. To enjoy the view while listening to the wild wind and the squeak of the pikas, visit Forest Canyon Overlook at dawn or dusk. At that time of day, deer and elk may be grazing on the tundra. Remember to bring binoculars and warm jackets. The first are advisable, but the latter are necessary because of the chilling wind that blows almost constantly at this altitude.

37

Sundance Mountain

DIFFICULTY: moderate
DISTANCE: 0.5 mile one way
USAGE: low
STARTING ELEVATION: 12,000 feet; elevation gain,
    446 feet
BACKCOUNTRY CAMPSITE: none
SEASON: summer, early fall
MAP: USGS 7.5-minute Trail Ridge

This is a steep, albeit very short hike that takes you to a rise above Trail Ridge Road. From the rounded peak of Sundance Mountain (actually more like a bump), the views are spectacular. This is a fine hike if time is limited or for a child's first climb.

Dress warmly, for it is not unusual for the tundra wind to blow over 30 miles per hour in the summer. Because of the wind-chill factor, a wind of that speed can lower the average 50-degree summer temperature to 28 degrees! Winter winds on Sundance Mountain often reach 70 to 100 miles per hour.

Drive to Deer Ridge Junction, as described in Hike 34. Continue on Trail Ridge Road (US Highway 34) 1.3 miles past Forest Canyon Overlook (if you are approaching from the west, Sundance Mountain is 4.8 miles east of the Alpine Visitor Center). Park at a small turnout on the south side of the highway. Sundance Mountain is visible to the east, across the highway. There is no trailhead sign.

There is no trail up Sundance Mountain; simply choose a route across the treeless tundra. It is impossible to get lost because Trail Ridge Road and the parking area are visible at all times. After topping a false summit, the peak of Sundance Mountain is also always in view. Rather than heading straight up, choose a moderate route that traverses the mountain. Whenever possible, walk on the rocks rather than the alpine plants.

The brevity of the hike provides time to enjoy the spectacular views. Far to the west rise the Never Summer Mountains, with Mount Richthofen (12,940 feet) rising dramatically above the other peaks of that range. Closer in, look southwest to Forest Canyon and the many peaks rising above it, among them Mount Ida (12,880) and the rounded Terra Tomah Mountain (12,718). To the southeast is the squared summit of Longs Peak (14,255) and its lumpy eastern neighbor, Twin Sisters Peaks (11,428). To the north is an excellent view of the Mummy Range.

This hike also provides an excellent opportunity to observe how glaciers created the dramatic topography of the park. The Ice Ages began approximately 1 million years ago. During this era, year-round temperatures that averaged well below freezing kept heavy snowfalls from melting in the summer. Mammoth snowdrifts compacted into ice, forming huge ice masses in protected areas near mountaintops. As more snow fell, the ice masses, or glaciers, grew into huge tongues of ice 1,000 to 1,500 feet thick.

Gravity pulled these glaciers down mountains and valleys. Embedded in the glaciers were tons of rock that gouged valley bottoms and steepened valley walls. Successive glaciers scoured the gentle slopes of the mountains, carving the rugged, precipitous peaks that now rise above Forest Canyon. You can envision the path and size of these glaciers by imagining that the dense

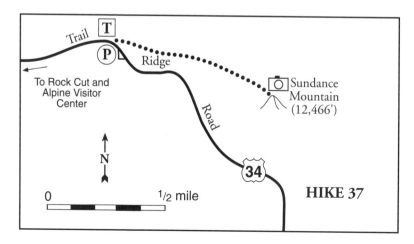

green forest of fir and spruce that covers the canyon to treeline is instead a mass of snow, ice, and rock traveling down the valley. Since the end of the last Ice Age, approximately 15,000 years ago, conifers have taken over where the glaciers once reigned.

Mount Ida and neighboring Terra Tomah Mountain are a study in glacial contrast. Rounded Terra Tomah Mountain escaped the glacial carving that created the pyramidal shape of Mount Ida. To see this contrast even more dramatically, compare the gentle, unglaciated western slope of Sundance Mountain with the peak's steep, glaciated northern flank. Look over the northern edge of the summit to see how steeply the mountain drops off.

Keep children under close supervision. The modern forces of wind, snow, and ice continue to do the work that the glaciers began. Rock continues to fall from the north side of the mountain to create an ever steeper and more precipitous drop.

The changes in alpine topography are slow and subtle compared to the annual riot of tundra flowers. The short growing season of the alpine zone, less than half that of a more temperate region, nevertheless creates a garden of great variety and rare and delicate beauty. Imagine mountains as spectators; each short season of alpine flowers is like a fireworks display—nearly as bright and just as quickly extinguished.

38

Tundra Trail at Rock Cut

DIFFICULTY: nature stroll, handicapped access with
    assistance
DISTANCE: 0.5 mile one way
USAGE: high
STARTING ELEVATION: 12,050 feet; elevation gain,
    260 feet
BACKCOUNTRY CAMPSITE: none
SEASON: summer, early fall
MAP: USGS 7.5-minute Trail Ridge

This trail ascends a flowered tundra slope to reach a fascinating rock formation with superior views. Along the path are informative

Rybergia (alpine sunflower)

signs interpreting the natural features seen along the way. At the top there is a peak finder that identifies the mountains that entirely surround you. The paved trail is wonderful for those in wheelchairs and for the parents of small children.

Rock Cut is located on Trail Ridge Road 2.1 miles west of Forest Canyon Overlook and 4 miles east of the Alpine Visitor Center. The trailhead has a large parking area and comfort stations.

This trail is one of the park's most popular walks. In midsummer, the path is crowded, and the parking lot is lined with tour buses. Take this trail in the early morning, when the winds are calmest and the crowds have not yet arrived. After the hike, stop at the nearby Alpine Visitor Center for a cup of hot chocolate. Dusk is another excellent time for this hike; people are few and the sunsets are spectacular. At dawn or dusk there is a good chance of seeing deer or elk on the ride up Trail Ridge Road.

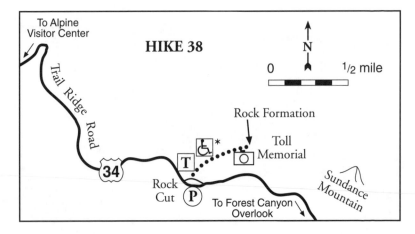

The path climbs gently for 0.5 mile to the Toll Memorial, which is located on a rocky bump of Sundance Mountain. The memorial honors Roger Toll, superintendent of the park from 1921 to 1929.

Despite the apparent similarity of the terrain, the trail actually passes several different tundra habitats, each of which supports uniquely adapted plants. The habitats include rocky fellfields, home to cushion plants such as pink moss campion; alpine turfs, which support American Bistort and Rydbergia; snowbed communities, where snow buttercup and clover-leaved rose can bloom after the late snow melts; and gopher gardens, where yellow alpine evens and blue sky pilot thrive in soil churned and fertilized by pocket gophers.

All these tundra plants are small, generally only a few inches tall. Contrary to what children might guess, these tiny plants are not young. Rather, they are fully formed, mature plants that may be decades old. A fist-sized cushion of moss campion, for example, is probably 25 years old or more! Moss campion does not even produce its first blossoms until it is ten years old.

Try a simple experiment with your children. Show them how alpine flowers hug the ground and barely raise their heads above the surface. Then let your children pretend they are tundra flowers. Ask them to crouch down or, even better, lie down on the trail. They will feel a noticeable difference in the temperature close to the ground, for wind speed increases with its distance above the surface. Increased wind velocity, of course, brings greater wind chill and colder temperatures. Alpine plants seek to escape the wind because it robs them of heat and precious moisture, and it tears at them with blowing dirt, ice, and snow.

Next, find a comparatively fast-growing Rydbergia, or alpine sunflower, a yellow composite that is the largest, showiest, and one of the most common of all the park's alpine wildflowers. Now ask your children to stand and turn away from the strong, cold wind. They will notice that they are more comfortable with their backs to the wind. So too with the Rydbergia, which almost always faces east, away from the prevailing westerly wind. Try using this flower as a natural compass.

If children realize that a plant no bigger than one of their fingers has taken their entire lifetimes just to store up enough energy to produce blossoms no bigger than a fingernail, and that the plant must survive ten months of winter each year with winds over 100 miles per hour, the children may look upon such a plant with new respect. You may even see them jump from rock to rock to avoid crushing the alpine flowers on subsequent trips to the tundra.

Tundra Trail at Rock Cut

The trail's first paved turnoff to the right leads to the peak finder at Toll Memorial. The views from the memorial are magnificent. The peak finder identifies mountains as far as 65 miles away. Here too are giant mushroom rocks, geological curiosities that are said to include some of the oldest rocks in the park. The dark heads of the "mushrooms" are over a billion years old.

Farther up the main path, a second rock outcropping to the right provides some climbing for older youngsters. The need to supervise is obvious. The view from the top of these rocks is again spectacular.

Back at the parking lot, carefully cross Trail Ridge Road to look at the rocky slope on the other side of the highway. On sunny days look among the rocks for yellow-bellied marmots and pikas. Look overhead and on the fence railings for the nattily attired black-billed magpie, in formal black and white, and the fluffy robin-sized gray jay.

This trail is a good introduction to more adventurous tundra hikes. If you enjoyed this walk in the "land above the trees," choose another hike from this section for a more intimate encounter.

39

Marmot Point

DIFFICULTY: easy
DISTANCE: 0.5 mile one way
USAGE: moderate
STARTING ELEVATION: 11,589 feet; elevation gain,
     320 feet
BACKCOUNTRY CAMPSITE: none
SEASON: summer, early fall
MAP: USGS 7.5-minute Trail Ridge

This short hike to the top of Marmot Point is a pleasant way to experience the alpine tundra and to stretch your legs after the long ride up Old Fall River Road. This walk, however, sticks close to the road and therefore lacks some of the beauty and serenity of other tundra hikes. Nevertheless, Marmot Point offers magnificent views and a chance to see wildflowers and wildlife.

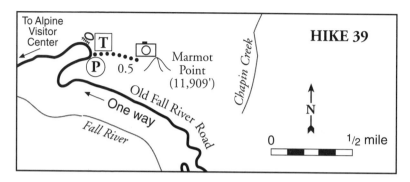

Drive Old Fall River Road, as described in Hike 24, 1.4 miles past the Chapin Creek Trailhead to a turnout on the right side of the road at Marker 24, just 0.5 mile east of the Alpine Visitor Center (AVC). The turnout is just before a fenced area containing the AVC's water treatment pond. Marmot Point is the cone-shaped peak east of the road. Or drive Trail Ridge Road to the AVC and hike down Old Fall River Road 0.5 mile (elevation loss, 200 feet).

The hike begins by heading up an old roadbed to an unused parking area. A footpath begins from the uphill side of the lot but soon disappears, leaving you to choose your own route to the top of Marmot Point.

In midsummer numerous alpine wildflowers cover the slope. The best way to see the tiny, brightly colored blooms is to crouch down to their level. Many are no larger than a dime. Their variety and intensity of color, however, more than compensate for their diminutive size. It is a miracle that any flowers can survive on this slope given the fleeting and tenuous eight-week growing season. It has been said that there are two seasons on the tundra: winter and the Fourth of July.

The clarity of the air and brightness of the light make the colors of the flowers appear more intense and make the surrounding mountains stand out sharply in detail. There is 25 percent more light at this altitude than at sea level, so distant objects appear deceptively near. The cool tundra air also seems fresher than the air at lower elevations. It is filled with smells of newly melted and newly fallen snow. It seems precious too as you gasp for more of it, while climbing up this relatively gentle slope. The air contains less oxygen than at sea level, so your heart and lungs must work harder.

Yellow-bellied marmot

This is a good hike to look for alpine wildlife. Scan the slopes for white-tailed ptarmigan, a grouse that lives above treeline. Indeed, the male is the only bird that lives on the tundra year-round (females winter below treeline). You need sharp eyes to spot a ptarmigan, for they are almost perfectly camouflaged in their summer plumage of brown and white. The birds are adept at locating each other, however, for ptarmigans are monogamous, re-uniting with the same mates each spring.

Look too for the elusive pika. This small, round-eared relative of the rabbit may be seen gathering plants to store for the winter. During the short tundra summer, pikas must gather enough greenery to last for nine or ten cold and barren months. The pika is one of the few mammals who remain active on the tundra in the winter, albeit mostly beneath the protective cover of rock piles.

Watch also for the namesake of this hill, the yellow-bellied marmot. This endearing western woodchuck is most often seen on sunny days, warming itself on the rocks. Unlike the pika, marmots prepare for winter by eating themselves to shiny-furred chubbiness. They live off their accumulated fat while they hibernate in rocky dens until spring.

The ropelike mounds of soil on the slopes of Marmot Point are the work of the seldom-seen pocket gopher. As an earth mover the pocket gopher is almost unequaled. In a single night the gopher can tunnel more than 100 feet! Imagine a network of tunnels roughly 1 foot beneath the surface of the ground, dug through rocky, half-frozen soil with teeth and claws in complete darkness. Not even earthworms brave the soil at this altitude.

Using binoculars, scan the slopes below the Alpine Visitor Center for grazing elk. You may be surprised to see quite a few elk among the trees.

Marmot Point offers views east and north to the gentle western slopes of the Mummy Range. There are also good views into the valleys of Chapin Creek and Fall River.

40

Fall River Pass Tundra Trail

DIFFICULTY: easy
DISTANCE: 0.25 mile one way
USAGE: high
STARTING ELEVATION: 11,796 feet; elevation gain,
      209 feet
BACKCOUNTRY CAMPSITE: none
SEASON: summer, early fall
MAP: USGS 7.5-minute Fall River Pass

A short but steep trail from the Alpine Visitor Center (AVC) climbs to a fine vantage point from which to view the spectacular Trail Ridge scenery. This well-used path at the busy visitor center is usually crowded and windy, but the short walk is worth the effort. Combine this walk with a visit to the AVC exhibits or one of the many activities available at the center.

The Alpine Visitor Center is located on Trail Ridge Road 17.1 miles from Deer Ridge Junction and 21 miles from the Grand Lake Entrance Station.

The trail begins just west of the Fall River Store, climbing a set of stairs set into the slope. Keep on the path; the tundra is already badly trampled in this area. Because of the slow growth of tundra plants, it will take several hundred years for this damaged area to recover.

Fall River Pass Tundra Trail

In summer, minute tundra wildflowers grace the slope. Take a moment to look for them among the rocks. These small plants hug the ground to escape the chilling, desiccating winds.

The top of the rise brings an awe-inspiring 360-degree view. To the west is the Never Summer Range with its permanent snowfields; to the north are Wyoming's Medicine Bow Mountains, 44 miles away; immediately to the east is the Mummy Range; and to the south, Forest Canyon lies more than 2,000 feet below. On the west side of Forest Canyon rise the dramatic peaks of the Continental Divide.

Watch also for deer or elk in the Chapin Creek Valley to the east. The grasses and shrubs of the valley make it prime habitat. Binoculars are helpful. Look also for brown-capped rosy finches. The small bird spends summers on the tundra and winters at lower elevations.

After reaching the high point in the trail, descend slightly to an observation platform to the west for more fine views. A sign indicates the role of the glaciers in sculpting this scenery. Sixty square miles of tundra stretch out before you. Take a moment to enjoy the superlative sights. Rocky Mountain National Park contains the largest expanse of protected tundra south of Alaska.

As you appreciate the expansive view from this platform, observe the exceptional quality of the air. According to the Park Service, visibility during the summer is usually at least 85 miles, while on some days visibility may be over 150 miles. Occasionally, however, visibility is impaired by manmade pollution. Most of the pollution that reduces air quality in the park comes from industrial regions in the Southwest, as far away as Southern California, Arizona, and New Mexico. A monitoring site for atmospheric visibility is located a few miles east of here, at the Gore Range Overlook. At this site, the effects of pollution are monitored to determine the extent of regional emissions.

41

Fall River Pass to Forest Canyon Pass

DIFFICULTY: easy
DISTANCE: 1.9 miles one way
USAGE: low
STARTING ELEVATION: 11,796 feet; elevation loss,
        476 feet
BACKCOUNTRY CAMPSITE: none
SEASON: summer, early fall
MAP: USGS 7.5-minute Fall River Pass

This short walk offers fabulous views and a nearly effortless entry into the alpine environment. Because the elevation gain is slight, it is easily managed by children. Deer and elk may be seen near Forest Canyon Pass.

Drive to the Alpine Visitor Center, as described in Hike 40. The trail begins across the street from the center and follows the former bed of the Old Fall River Road, which was built in the early 1900s and was replaced by Trail Ridge Road in 1934. Fortunately for hikers, the section of the old road from Fall River Pass to Milner Pass has been allowed to return to tundra.

Sounds of birds and the ever-present rushing wind make busy Trail Ridge Road seem far away even at the start of this hike. The wind is a critical factor in determining the look and feel of the tundra.

Its work is evident in the diminutive height of all tundra plants, which hug the ground for warmth and to escape the desiccating and chilling wind. Barren patches of rock, where the wind has stripped the surface bare of soil, are common. In winter the wind can howl across the peaks at over 200 miles per hour. Even in summer it is not unusual to encounter winds of 40 miles per hour. Yet the wind is also life-giving, scattering the seeds and pollen of the alpine plants.

In summer a wide variety of wildflowers grace this trail, including alpine evens, western yellow paintbrush, moss campion, alpine clover, and Rydbergia, or alpine sunflower.

Also look for the white-tailed ptarmigan, a common tundra inhabitant that is extremely difficult to spot. The perfect camouflage of this small grouse makes it nearly invisible among the rocks and grasses. If you see a ptarmigan, look for chicks following the adult.

The trail offers tremendous views. To the west is a spectacular view of the Never Summer Mountains. Perpetual snowbanks on their eastern slopes inspired the Arapaho to name the range *Ne-chibe-chii,* translated as "Never-No-Summer."

A short distance down the trail, pass the first of a series of five small ponds. In the mud by the water, look for the tracks of deer and elk. Elk tracks are easy to distinguish by their longer, wider, and more rounded appearance. An elk track measures approximately 4½ by 3 inches, while those of a deer are only 3 by 2¾ inches and are more heart-shaped.

Look into the ponds for the tiny, almost transparent fairy shrimp darting about in the water, its ten legs propelling it here and there erratically. By parthenogenesis (reproduction without

Hikers near Fall River Pass

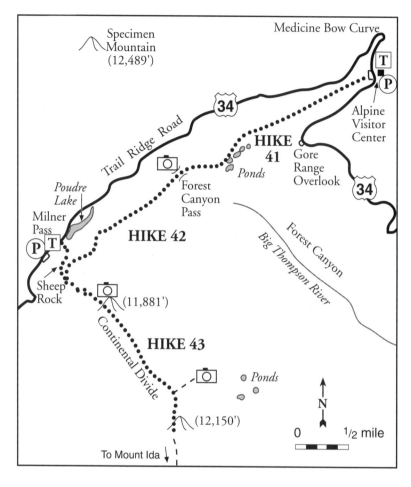

the opposite sex) as well as fertilization, the prehistoric-looking fairy shrimp produces winter eggs with a shell thick enough to endure the freezing of its pond.

After passing the ponds, reach Forest Canyon Pass, where chances are good of seeing elk and deer in the patches of small, gnarled trees known as *krummholz*. During the day the animals retreat to the *krummholz* for cover. Deer and elk usually feed at dawn or dusk.

Forest Canyon Pass features a superb view into spruce-covered, glacially carved Forest Canyon. Originally, the valley was a deep, narrow, V-shaped canyon eroded about 28 million years ago by the

ancestor of the Big Thompson River. During the subsequent Ice
Ages, immense walls of ice, 1,000 to 1,500 feet thick, flowed slowly
from the mountains down this valley. The huge slug of ice carved
the canyon into its present U-shaped configuration, broadening
the floor of the valley and steepening its sides. This U shape is
characteristic of glacially formed valleys and can be seen else-
where in the park, notably in Spruce Canyon and the Kawuneeche
Valley. From Forest Canyon Pass, retrace your steps to the
trailhead.

HIKING OPTIONS:
   Combine this hike with Hike 42 for a one-way trip of 4.2 miles.

42

Milner Pass to Forest Canyon Pass

DIFFICULTY: moderate
DISTANCE: 2.3 miles one way
USAGE: low
STARTING ELEVATION: 10,750 feet; elevation gain,
      530 feet
BACKCOUNTRY CAMPSITE: none
SEASON: summer, fall
MAP: USGS 7.5-minute Fall River Pass

This very scenic hike leads above treeline to Forest Canyon Pass,
where the views of Forest Canyon and the surrounding peaks are
spectacular. The trail travels from subalpine forest to the tundra,
passing through two dramatically different life zones. It is an
excellent trail for sighting deer, elk, and the wildlife of the subalpine forest.
   Milner Pass Trailhead is located at the south end of Poudre
Lake. From the Alpine Visitor Center, drive Trail Ridge Road (US
Highway 34) 4.3 miles southwest to the trailhead, where parking is available. From the Grand Lake Entrance Station, drive US
Highway 34 for 16.7 miles to the trailhead.
   The hike begins on the smooth, well-trodden path around the
south end of Poudre Lake. The rise in elevation is gradual at
first. The trail then steepens and climbs toward the interesting

rock formation of Sheep Rock, a half mile from the trailhead. The rock has been so named because of the presence of bighorn sheep in the area, primarily in the summer. Their breeding ground is on the west side of Specimen Mountain, just northwest of the Milner Pass Trailhead. Specimen Mountain, which rises to 12,489 feet, is clearly visible from most sections of the trail.

Please do not approach or harass bighorn sheep. They are extremely susceptible to stress, and the fear of an approaching hiker can actually cause them physical harm. If you are lucky enough to encounter a bighorn on the trail, remain still and silent. The bighorn is a curious animal and, if not frightened, may even approach you!

After Sheep Rock, a rock cairn on the right marks a trail that climbs steeply to the south. This trail leads to the Continental Divide and is described in Hike 43. Stay to the left.

Thus far the trail has passed through a forest of subalpine fir and Engelmann spruce. The two conifers are easily distinguished by feeling their needles. A subalpine fir has flat needles that are rounded at the end and soft to the touch. The needles of the spruce, on the other hand, are more or less square in cross-section and sharp at the tip. To remember the spruce, associate the "s" of spruce with sharp and square. In Rocky Mountain National Park, subalpine forest occurs between altitudes of 9,000 and 11,500 feet.

By trapping great quantities of snow, the subalpine forest creates a moist environment. Consequently a wide variety of moisture-loving flowers are found here in the summer, including yellow monkeyflowers and marsh marigolds, white mountain figwort, and tall blue chimingbells. Broom huckleberry, a variety of wild blueberry, provides extensive ground cover in the subalpine forest, carpeting the forest floor in late summer with sweet berries. Also look for subalpine Jacob's ladder, whose flowers are dainty blue and whose leaves have a skunklike aroma when crushed.

During this portion of the hike, be alert for wildlife. While enjoying a snack on one of the downed trees by the trail, watch for golden-mantled ground squirrels and chipmunks, both of which are common here. Far less often seen are weasels and snowshoe hares. You may hear but not see scolding chickarees, or red squirrels, who will most likely be hidden from view high in a tree. Another, more visible scold is Clark's nutcracker, a handsome, gray relative of jays and crows, with black and white wings and a sharp, awl-shaped beak. Its loud dissonant squawking is a familiar sound in the subalpine forest. Other common, more melodious birds of the forest include the fluffy gray jay and the gray-headed junco.

Approximately 1 mile from the trailhead, the trail widens to an old roadbed, where the hiking is easy. The track is all that remains of the western half of the Old Fall River Road, which was built in the early 1900s. The road was in use until 1932, when it was replaced by Trail Ridge Road. The steep eastern section of Old Fall River Road is still maintained and makes an interesting drive.

Climbing toward Forest Canyon Pass, notice how the trees become progressively shorter with elevation. At this altitude the growing seasons are so short that a tree that stands no taller than a 4-foot-tall child may be more than 400 years old. The gnarled, shrubby clumps of firs and spruces that grow near the pass are known as *krummholz,* a German word meaning "crooked wood." The *krummholz* zone is the area right below treeline where trees struggle to survive under tremendously adverse conditions. Strong wind, low temperatures, and blowing snow bombard the trees, stunting their growth and distorting their shape. The trees survive because they tolerate low temperatures and are able to grow close to the ground, where they trap moisture and partially escape the desiccating and destructive winds. Trees on the windward side of a *krummholz* clump provide protection for those in the center and on the leeward side. As the windward trees in the clump die off, the protected trees in their lee extend the clump by layering (i.e., limbs that touch the ground sprout new roots).

The *krummholz* is a favorite habitat for mule deer and elk. In the summer, herds of elk retreat to this area to escape the heat of the lower elevations. The plants growing in and around the *krummholz* provide choice food. The tree islands also provide cover from the winds and cold of the tundra, as well as from the tourists traveling on Trail Ridge Road. Hike this area in the early morning or at dusk for a chance to see the animals feeding.

Continue a short distance above the *krummholz* to Forest Canyon Pass, a magnificent place to explore. The view from the pass is incredible. Mountains and green valleys are visible in all directions, but the peaks of the Continental Divide and the Never Summer Range dominate the scene.

But the superlative view is not the sole reward of this hike. The tundra is a land of surprises. From a distance it looks gray and barren, but upon closer examination, it is rich with color, diversity, and drama. In the summer, tiny flowers carpet the tundra with multicolored miniature blossoms. With the exception of cold temperatures, growing conditions on the tundra are comparable to those on a desert. In both habitats, plants have to endure insufficient and erratic moisture, intense sun, strong winds, and high evaporation rates. The growing season above treeline is considerably colder and briefer than at lower, more temperate elevations. It lasts only six to eight weeks, during which time the average high temperature is only 50 degrees. For five months of the year the temperature does not climb above 32 degrees.

HIKING OPTIONS:

(1) An interesting short extension to this hike is to walk a half mile farther on the trail to a series of ponds just off the trail. The ponds are visible from Forest Canyon Pass. In the mud surrounding the ponds, elk and deer tracks can be clearly seen. In addition, the ponds contain the prehistoric-looking, almost-too-tiny-to-see fairy shrimp. (2) The trail from Milner Pass continues all the way to the Alpine Visitor Center. The center is 1.9 miles from Forest Canyon Pass (Hike 41). The whole trail is best done (downhill) from the center to Milner Pass. The round-trip distance to the center from the Milner Pass Trailhead is 8.4 miles, with an elevation gain of 1,038 feet.

43

Milner Pass Along the Continental Divide

DIFFICULTY: strenuous
DISTANCE: 2.1 miles one way
USAGE: low
STARTING ELEVATION: 10,750 feet; elevation gain,
    1,400 feet
BACKCOUNTRY CAMPSITE: none
SEASON: summer, early fall
MAP: USGS 7.5-minute Fall River Pass

This spectacular high-country hike offers exceptional views on a short but very steep trail. For children (and their parents), there are marmots, pikas, deer, and elk. This hike is a good introduction to the "land above the trees" for older youngsters who don't mind a little bit of tough hiking.

Drive to Milner Pass Trailhead, as described in Hike 42. The hike begins on the Ute Trail. After 0.8 mile, look for a rock cairn on the right that marks the spur trail leading along the Continental Divide. From this point, the trail heads south. This trail is considerably steeper and narrower than the one just left. Fortunately, treeline is not far away. After approximately a half mile of switchbacks, you reach treeline, on the west side of an unnamed 11,881-foot peak. South of this peak, the hiking is divine as the trail easily traverses a series of unnamed ridges and bumps.

The views along this traverse are worth the effort. The Never Summer Mountains are to the west, Specimen Mountain (12,489 feet) rises to the north, and the trail leads south to Mount Ida (12,880 feet). With such clear landmarks, and with the trail nearly always in view, it is possible to safely hike cross-country and explore. An excellent off-trail destination is the ridge just south of Point 11,881, on the Continental Divide. Walk carefully across the tundra to the top of this ridge. To minimize impact, remember to walk side by side rather than single file, tread lightly, and step on rocks wherever possible. From the ridge, you can see hundreds of feet downslope to a group of unnamed ponds set among *krummholz*. The ponds are often visited by elk in summer. A pair of binoculars will help you find the elk.

Back on the trail, hiking continues to be easy until you reach a second unnamed peak (12,150 feet), approximately 2.1 miles from the trailhead. After this point, the going gets tough as the trail becomes faint or nonexistent and traverses the slope amid loose rock. To add to the difficulty, the grade of the slope steepens considerably. This portion of the hike is not advisable for children and is best attempted by those bent on reaching the tough, but worthwhile goal of Mount Ida (12,880 feet), 2 miles away.

On the way back to the trailhead, look for yellow-bellied marmots sunning themselves on the rocks. According to one park ranger, marmots are born "retired." They spend their days lazily eating, sleeping, and resting in the sun, content simply to watch the world go by.

Also inhabiting the rocky areas of the high country are the pikas. In contrast to the marmots, these small, round-eared

Hiker and gopher garlands on the Continental Divide

relatives of the rabbit are shy and industrious. Unlike marmots, pikas do not hibernate and therefore need a large supply of food for the long winter. Throughout the summer pikas scurry across the rocks, gathering plants and grasses for their winter food supply. They spread out the greenery on the rocks to dry. When the hay is ready, the pikas then store it in piles beneath the rocks.

Also look for evidence of pocket gophers in the form of serpentine gopher garlands. These long, narrow ropelike mounds are the vestiges of tunnels that gophers dig under the snow in the winter. The disturbed and fertilized soil is thought to provide a good seedbed for tundra flowers.

CHAPTER

4

West Side Hikes

The hikes in this section are located west of the Continental Divide. All are within easy driving distance of Grand Lake. The west side of the park is delightfully quieter than the east, and the trails are likely to be far less crowded. The west side is also generally cooler, wetter, and more lushly vegetated. Although west-side vistas are generally less dramatic than those of the east, its trails are well worth visiting. In spring and fall, wildlife abounds in the Kawuneeche Valley. If you are traveling from the east side to the west side, check for local variations in weather. It may be cool and rainy on the west side when the eastern slope is basking in warm sunshine.

44

Poudre River Trail

DIFFICULTY: easy
DISTANCE: 1 to 2.5 miles one way
USAGE: low
STARTING ELEVATION: 10,750 feet; elevation gain,
      160 feet
BACKCOUNTRY CAMPSITES: none
SEASON: summer, fall
MAP: USGS 7.5-minute Fall River Pass

This hike beside the Cache la Poudre River is a pleasant, meandering journey with no specific goal. It is simply an enjoyable, almost level walk that leads briefly through subalpine forest to the wet, rich deer and elk habitat along the Poudre River. At dawn or dusk the chances of seeing deer and elk are excellent. Try this hike as an early morning excursion, after which you can get a hot chocolate at the Alpine Visitor Center and refuel for another hike. At any hour, the Poudre River Trail is a relaxing, uncrowded hike ideal for spontaneous exploring.

The trailhead is located on the west side of Trail Ridge Road, 4 miles southwest of the Alpine Visitor Center and 17 miles north of the Grand Lake Entrance Station. From the Beaver Meadows Entrance Station, the trailhead is 24 miles west on Trail Ridge Road. Park at a turnout on the west side of the road, 0.1 mile north of the parking lot for the Crater (Hike 45).

The Cache la Poudre River was named by French fur trappers, who hid a quantity of gunpowder beside the river in the fall of 1836. Returning in the spring for the powder, the trappers found their cache, and thereafter referred to the river as the hiding place for the powder—*cache la poudre.*

The hike starts on a narrow trail through a subalpine forest of Engelmann spruce and subalpine fir. You can easily learn to tell the difference between these two conifers by feeling their needles. If the needles feel sharp, they belong to the spruce; if the needles feel soft, they belong to the fir. In late summer, look on the forest floor for the sweet berries of the broom huckleberry. Look also for wildflowers, including yellow monkeyflowers, white mountain figwort (parrot's beak), and tall blue chimingbells. The names of these flowers graphically (and imaginatively) describe their appearance. See if your children can find these flowers based on their creative names.

After approximately 0.25 mile, the trail leaves the forest to follow the marshy drainage of the Cache la Poudre River. Here the trail is pleasant but occasionally wet as it meanders next to the river and crosses numerous small streams. Notice how the plants and flowers change as the trail approaches and leaves the banks of the river. US Highway 34 is unfortunately just across the narrow valley, and although the road is obscured by trees, car noises may be audible. Early in the morning, however, traffic and noise are negligible.

Look for signs of deer and elk as you walk along the willow-lined trail. Their prints are visible in the moist soil. Elk tracks are easy to distinguish from deer tracks, for elk tracks are larger, wider, and more rounded, measuring approximately 4½ by 3 inches. A deer track is smaller and more heart-shaped, usually only 3 by 2¾ inches. Deer and elk generally graze or browse at dawn and dusk, retreating to the safety of the forest during the day and at night.

The American elk, or wapiti, is an impressive animal. Bulls reach 5 feet at the shoulder and weigh 750 pounds. A mature bull's antlers can span 5 feet and weigh 25 pounds. In summer, elk are reddish-brown on their sides, with a large yellow-white rump patch, and dark brown neck. In fall, their coat turns a darker gray-brown. If you are lucky enough to sight a herd of elk close up, you will not forget it.

Large herds of elk once ranged across the entire United States, from the Atlantic to the Pacific, Canada to Mexico. After the European invasion of the continent, however, the elk population declined dramatically. By 1800 the eastern elk herds were completely gone as a result of market hunting and loss of habitat. By 1900, elk survived in the Rockies only in isolated locations. In fact, the current healthy population of elk in Rocky Mountain National Park descends from animals imported from Yellowstone National Park in the 1930s.

Mule deer are considerably smaller than elk. Males stand 3.5 feet at the shoulder and weigh 250 pounds. The deer are reddish-tan in summer and grayish-brown in winter, with a small white rump patch and black-tipped white tail. Their large, mulelike ears are extremely sensitive and can move independently, endowing the deer with a superior sense of hearing. You are likely to see many mule deer throughout the park if you are up early or out at dusk. During the summer, does are frequently seen with their twin spotted fawns, provoking squeals of delight from children who are familiar with Bambi.

Walk as far as you wish along the river. In wet seasons a muddy trail might precipitate an early retreat. Before returning to the trailhead, you may want to ask your children to think like a deer or an elk and tell you why they would choose to live in this valley. Perhaps they will mention the easily accessible water; the wealth of food in the form of grasses, flowers, shrubs, and small trees; the cover provided by the forest in times of danger; the

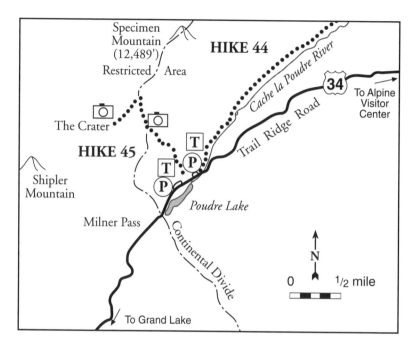

shade of the trees in summer; or the undergrowth where camouflaged fawns can hide.

45

The Crater

DIFFICULTY: moderate
DISTANCE: 1 mile one way
USAGE: moderate
STARTING ELEVATION: 10,750 feet; elevation gain,
    730 feet
BACKCOUNTRY CAMPSITE: none
SEASON: summer, fall
MAP: USGS 7.5-minute Fall River Pass

The trail to the Crater is one of the finest short hikes in the park.
It offers verdant subalpine forest, spectacular alpine scenery, and

Hikers on top of The Crater

a chance to see one of the most magnificent and elusive of the park's large mammals, the bighorn sheep. The trail travels near their lambing and feeding grounds on the tundra of Specimen Mountain.

Bighorn sheep are particularly sensitive to human disturbance. They generally inhabit remote sections of the park, far from man and other predators, often on precipitous slopes high above treeline. Harassing or even unintentionally startling these sensitive creatures can seriously harm them. For example, fear of approaching humans can generate such stress in the sheep that they suffer cardiac arrest. Repeated stress makes the sheep less resistant to diseases that plague the herds and consequently will reduce their numbers. The bighorn population in the park is already extremely fragile, numbering only 400 in 1998.

To protect the sheep during vital lambing periods, the Park Service prohibits all hiking on Specimen Mountain until midsummer (approximately July 1). After that date, limited access is provided by this trail, but the actual lambing area is always closed to hikers. Because of the fragility of the population, it is *critical* that you observe these restrictions.

The trailhead is located on the west side of Trail Ridge Road, 4.1 miles southwest from the Alpine Visitor Center and 16.9 miles north of the Grand Lake Entrance Station. From the Beaver Meadows Entrance Station, the trailhead is 24.1 miles west on

Trail Ridge Road. Parking is available at the trailhead. If the small lot is full, there is additional parking 0.1 mile north on Trail Ridge Road (US Highway 34).

From the trailhead, the trail begins in meadow but quickly enters a mature forest of subalpine fir and Engelmann spruce, switchbacking steeply as it heads for treeline and the open tundra, approximately two-thirds of a mile away. In the forest notice the variety of wildflowers that love the shade, moisture, and coolness of the subalpine forest. Among the more abundant wildflowers is white mountain figwort or "parrot's beak," whose blossom looks like the tiny hooked beak of a miniature white parrot. Look also for the blue mountain harebell, whose blossom hangs down from the stem like a tiny bell. Because of the flower's shape, the plant is also called a witch's thimble. The harebell is a delectable treat for the elk, deer, pikas, marmots, and sheep.

Another, more familiar edible crop is the delicate-leaved wild blueberry which covers the forest floor. It produces a blue bloom in early summer and sweet berries in August. Be sure to leave an ample supply for the park's few black bears, which particularly favor them.

One of the most easily identified flowers is the Indian paintbrush, which resembles a small green brush dipped in red or yellow paint.

Proceeding through the forest, watch for squirrel middens consisting of large piles of cone scales and discarded cores, which have been gathered and eaten by red squirrels (chickarees). Beneath such piles of refuse are likely to be large caches of pine cones.

The first views through breaks in the trees are of impressive Specimen Mountain (12,489 feet) to the north. After climbing a little higher, enjoy a more expansive view to the north and east. Trail Ridge Road, the Alpine Visitor Center, and the west side of the Mummy Range are all in sight. Also notice the verdant Cache La Poudre Valley, where a wealth of shrubs, grasses, and sedges creates a rich summer buffet for deer and elk (see Hike 44).

As you approach a rocky area near treeline, look for the Colorado blue columbine, one of the most beautiful of the park's flowers. The blossoms of the columbine, whose name is derived from the Latin *columba,* meaning "dove," were thought to look like circles of doves dancing around the stems. The Colorado blue columbine's inner layer of white petals do resemble the backs of doves, set off by the outer sepals of blue, which mimic the clear Colorado sky. Native Americans used a tea made from columbine leaves to cure fevers and headaches.

On the trail, look for tracks of deer and elk. At treeline, notice the long ropelike mounds of dirt left by pocket gophers. These energetic excavators can tunnel more than 100 feet in one night. The animal was named for its cheek pockets, which open to the outside instead of into its mouth. The pocket gopher gathers seeds in his cheeks and then empties his cheek pockets by turning them inside out, just as we would empty a pants pocket. Special muscles snap the pockets back into place.

Above treeline, the view west to the Never Summer Range is excellent and continues to improve as you climb higher. Follow the narrow path as it heads toward a saddle between Specimen Mountain and the Crater. At the saddle, a sign indicates the restricted lambing area. Find a comfortable perch here to watch for bighorn, or ascend to the top of the Crater on the faint trail to the left. Views from the top of the Crater are magnificent.

From either the Crater or the saddle, enjoy a good view to the northwest of Mount Richthofen (12,940 feet), the highest peak in the Never Summer Range. Below you to the west is the Kawuneeche Valley. The small mountain directly southwest of the Crater is Shipler Mountain.

If you see one sheep, you will probably see many. Rarely do bighorn sheep travel alone, for they are gregarious animals with a highly evolved social system. Look for sheep on the west side of the Crater and on the rocky western slopes of Specimen Mountain. Binoculars would be useful. In summer and fall the bighorns have dark brown coats and a large white rump patch and black tail. Rams can grow to 3.5 feet at the shoulder and may weigh up to 400 pounds; females are considerably smaller. Both males and females have horns that grow continuously throughout their lives. A healthy and mature ram's horn will reach a full and magnificent curl on each side of its head. A three-quarter curl indicates that a ram is approximately ten years old. In contrast, a ewe's horns are short and spiky, like those of a young ram.

During the fall mating season, rams compete for ewes by butting heads. The sound of the rock-solid horns slamming together can be heard a mile away. Despite the force of these cracks, dueling rams seldom hurt each other, and usually the smaller or weaker ram simply withdraws out of exhaustion.

Bighorn sheep are diurnal, so daytime hours are the best time to look for them. You are fortunate if you are able to observe these magnificent creatures. Though millions of bighorn sheep once roamed the Rockies, only small herds survive today, owing to extensive market hunting in the late 1800s, loss of habitat, and infection by diseases of domestic livestock.

46

Lulu City

DIFFICULTY: moderate
DISTANCE: 3.6 miles one way
USAGE: moderate
STARTING ELEVATION: 9,010 feet; elevation gain,
    350 feet
BACKCOUNTRY CAMPSITE: none
SEASON: summer, fall
MAP: USGS 7.5-minute Fall River Pass

This very pleasant, almost level walk along the Colorado River leads to the site of a mining boom town of the late 1800s. Although not much remains of Lulu City, the trail is rich with the ghosts of miners. Discover abandoned cabins, ruins, and mines, and for more inspiration, take along the well-written account of Lulu City, which is available at park visitor centers.

The Colorado River Trailhead is on the west side of US Highway 34, 10.5 miles north of the Grand Lake Entrance Station and 10.5 miles south of the Alpine Visitor Center. There is a parking lot at the trailhead.

This hike is a good choice if you are uncertain of the stamina of your group, for the following intermediate goals make good turnarounds: (1) the first abandoned mine (1.2 miles), (2) the cabin ruins and second mine (1.3 miles), (3) the Shipler Mine (2 miles), (4) the Shipler Cabin site (2.4 miles), or (5) the beginning of the old stage road (2.7 miles).

From the trailhead, the trail heads north and immediately climbs a short steep hill, but beyond the hill the trail is nearly level. For much of the way, the path is wide and smooth, allowing two people to stroll abreast. Many varieties of wildflowers line the trail, and the trees are alive with the sounds of birds and chattering red squirrels.

At 0.6 mile from the trailhead, the trail to Lulu City (La Poudre Pass Trail) splits from the Red Mountain Trail, which heads left. Take the right fork, which continues north along the east side of the Colorado River, almost always keeping within sight of the water and sometimes meandering right up to it. There are many good picnic spots along the river, and the bank makes a fascinating playground for youngsters.

The headwaters of the Colorado River lie 7 miles up the trail to the north at La Poudre Pass. This gentle singing stream is the start of the great river that carved the Grand Canyon and on which the entire Southwest relies. From this point in the Rockies, the river flows more than 1,400 miles to the Gulf of California.

After approximately 1.2 miles, a spur trail climbs steeply uphill to the right to an abandoned mine. This is one of the numerous mine shafts dug into Shipler Mountain, probably between 1870 and 1900. Do not enter the mine.

After returning to the trail, come to another set of paths, one leading to the right, another to the left. The path to the right leads to a second abandoned mine, this one boarded up and scarred with graffiti. The path to the left leads to cabin ruins, where there is evidence of a stone fireplace. Notice that the foundations of the cabins are remarkably small. Most of the houses built by prospectors were built hastily, often only seven logs high and roofed with poles and dirt. Most miners did not winter at their mining sites, but retreated to warmer, more populous areas until spring.

Shipler Mine is approximately 2 miles from the trailhead. The site is marked by a large tailings pile on the right. This rocky slope is an excellent place to see yellow-bellied marmots. These western woodchucks inhabit rocky areas and enjoy napping on the sun-warmed rocks. In late summer, wild raspberries ripen near the trail at the base of the tailings.

Shipler Mine is an interesting mine to visit. To reach its entrance, carefully climb the slope to the north of the tailings. Do not attempt to climb up the tailings, for the pile is unstable. Do not enter this mine without a park ranger. The Park Service runs guided hikes to the mine during the summer. For more information, check with the park visitor centers.

The trail to Lulu City

Continue down the trail 0.4 mile to the ruins of Joe Shipler's cabin, at the edge of a beautiful subalpine meadow. Joe Shipler, a miner, lived here with his family from 1876 until 1914. Comfort stations are located just behind the cabins.

Beyond the cabins, notice unhealed wagon-wheel ruts beside the trail, evidence of the stagecoach road that once brought mail, provisions, and hundreds of prospectors to Lulu City. Also notice the new tree growth on either side of the trail, indicating the swath of road that was cut almost 100 years ago.

At 3.4 miles, come to a trail junction. The right fork leads north to Little Yellowstone Canyon. Take the left fork to Lulu City, a short 0.2-mile downhill. On this last leg of the trail, walk through a fine stand of aspens, which are particularly beautiful in the fall.

At the site of Lulu City the trail opens up to a lovely flowered meadow—a wonderful picnic spot with safe, easy access to the river. Children will enjoy the chipmunks, golden-mantled ground squirrels, and gray jays. The meadow is bordered on the west by the picturesque peaks of the Never Summer Mountains. Toilet facilities are located after a small bridge.

Explore the undergrowth to find cabin foundations, tailings piles, and rusted pieces of machinery. Very little remains here of what was once a bustling boom town. It is hard to imagine that 100 square blocks were laid out, named, and marketed by ambitious city planners.

The dreams of those coming to Lulu City were as grand as the scenery. Dubbed "The Coming Metropolis of Grand County," the town thrived between 1880 and 1883, peaking at a population of 500. During this time, stagecoaches arrived five times weekly from Grand Lake and Fort Collins. A hotel with linen, silver, and fine china served well-to-do travelers. The town supported liquor, hardware, clothing, and grocery stores; two sawmills; and a two-cabin red-light district. But the mines at Lulu City produced only low-grade ore, which was unprofitable to mine in the absence of a nearby smelter. Consequently, Lulu City was largely abandoned by 1883.

Unfortunately, one of the most enduring signs of Lulu City's mining is the deposition of iron manganese precipitate (an orange deposit) along the banks of the Colorado River. Throughout Colorado, similar drainage from long-abandoned mines now endangers precious water sources. The state is currently seeking solutions to this dangerous legacy of its mining heritage.

47

Grand Ditch

DIFFICULTY: strenuous
DISTANCE: 3.4 miles one way
USAGE: low
STARTING ELEVATION: 9,010 feet; elevation gain,
    1,200 feet
BACKCOUNTRY CAMPSITE: 3.2 and 3.5 miles from the
    trailhead
SEASON: summer, fall
MAP: USGS 7.5-minute Fall River Pass

This uphill climb to the water diversion project of the Grand Ditch is a surprisingly scenic hike. The trail offers verdant forest, scenic

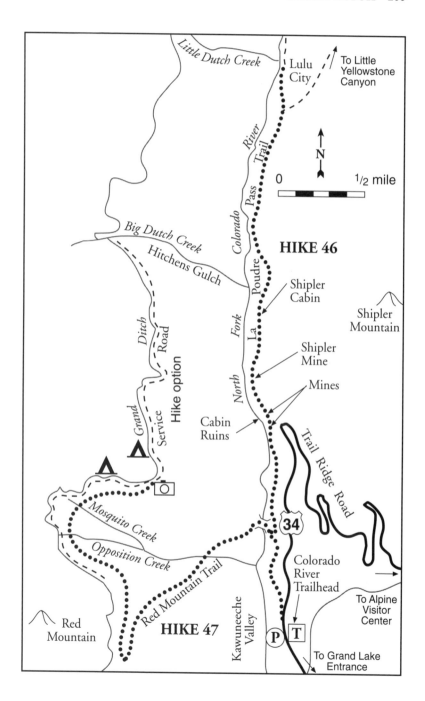

Little Dutch Creek

Lulu City

To Little Yellowstone Canyon

River Trail

N

0   1/2 mile

Colorado Pass

Big Dutch Creek

Hitchens Gulch

La Poudre

HIKE 46

Shipler Cabin

Shipler Mountain

Ditch Road

Shipler Mine

Grand

North Fork

Service

Hike option

Mines

Cabin Ruins

Trail Ridge Road

Mosquito Creek

34

Opposition Creek

Red Mountain Trail

Colorado River Trailhead

To Alpine Visitor Center

Red Mountain

HIKE 47

Kawuneeche Valley

P T

To Grand Lake Entrance

views, marmots, pikas, several small cascading streams, and a somewhat sobering lesson in water conservation. The service road next to the ditch provides an abundance of good views and a very easy walk high above the Kawuneeche Valley. In late summer, the trail is one of the best for sampling wild berries.

Drive to the Colorado River Trailhead, as described in Hike 46. From the trailhead, head north for an easy 0.6 mile to the junction with the Red Mountain Trail. Take the Red Mountain Trail west crossing the Colorado on a substantial bridge. After a pretty meadow, enter a mature subalpine forest, where the trail steepens. Climb for 0.2 mile to the first crossing of Opposition Creek, a very clear, fast-flowing stream.

The trail ascends moderately for another half mile, then crosses a rocky area, with views to the east of magnificent green mountain ridges. Aspen trees grow among the rocks, framing the views and making this section especially pretty in the fall. Throughout the summer, bright pink fireweed provides a stunning contrast to the gray rocks.

Aspens and fireweed are common to areas that have been disturbed by fire, rock slides, avalanches, or logging. Aspens regenerate themselves quickly from root networks that survive in the soil; when an opening in the forest is created, as by a fire, the roots generate new suckers, which form a new colony of aspens. Fireweed colonizes disturbed areas by means of seeds equipped with long silky threads, which act like parachutes in the wind. The paratrooping seeds invade after a natural disaster and quickly germinate in the bare soil. Fireweed's rapid growth helps hold the soil in place, thereby preventing erosion.

Native Americans enjoyed the taste of fireweed and, reportedly, Russians long ago used it to make beer. More locally significant, fireweed is a favorite food of the grizzly bear in the northern Rockies and of the elk in this park.

This rocky slope is a good place to rest, sample wild raspberries, and watch for marmots and pikas. Below is a fine view into the Kawuneeche Valley, through which the young Colorado River twists and turns.

Leave this rocky area to travel south, and then switchback north through a rich subalpine forest consisting of Engelmann spruce, subalpine fir, and aspen. The forest floor is colorful with purple and white wildflowers. Wild blueberries sport delicate blue flowers in midsummer and tiny purple berries at season's end. This fine forest walk offers diversity, dappled sunlight, songs of birds, and lush scents.

After another rocky and open area, the trail passes a small pond, home to a large variety of creeping, crawling delights for interested youngsters. Watch for water boatmen, whirligig beetles, and midges.

Beyond the pond, the path reenters forest and rises again. After crossing Opposition and Mosquito Creeks, continue uphill another 0.6 mile to the Grand Ditch. The views are fabulous. Walk along the service road in either direction. Just about 0.2 mile north, find a backcountry campsite west of the trail. To the south, aptly named Red Mountain rises dramatically. Mount Cumulus looms to the west, Howard and Lead Mountains to the north. The long Kawuneeche Valley is visible below. The nearly level road provides miles of effortless hiking. Those hiking southwest will find a campsite at the ditch, 3.5 miles from the trailhead. Although a sunrise would be magnificent from this spot, the uphill hike to the campsite with loaded packs would be very strenuous.

The Grand Ditch was an early attempt to divert large quantities of water to the arid lands east of the Continental Divide. The vast eastern prairies had rich soil but too little rainfall to sustain agriculture. Inventive farmers coveted the heavy snowfall on the western slopes of the mountains, whose meltwater flows west, not east. Their solution in 1890 was to build a diversion ditch to capture the melting snow and empty it into an east-flowing river. The ditch was begun at La Poudre Pass to catch water that ordinarily would have drained into the Colorado River. At its completion in 1936, the 20-foot wide, 6-foot deep ditch reached 14.3 miles.

The Grand Ditch had many effects. The scar on this mountain range is visible a great distance away, and severe erosion is evident on the slopes. The ditch also cut the flow of the North Fork of the Colorado River in half, adversely affecting the once thriving fish population.

It is now clear that irreversible loss of habitat, destruction of wilderness, erosion, and the loss of fish and wildlife may result from construction of dams, reservoirs, and water diversion projects. Given these risks, conservation is the only acceptable long-term solution. In Denver, single-family homes consume 65 percent of the water in the metropolitan area, and half of that amount is used to water lawns. The price for green grass, measured in lost wilderness, tamed rivers, and destroyed habitat, is too high.

HIKING OPTIONS:
   A good destination along the service road is Hitchens Gulch, 1.7 miles north. Wildflowers bloom along the Gulch, through which Big Dutch Creek runs east to meet the Colorado River.

48

Never Summer Ranch

DIFFICULTY: nature stroll, handicapped access with
         assistance (buildings are not accessible)
DISTANCE: 0.75 mile one way
USAGE: moderate
STARTING ELEVATION: 9,100 feet; elevation gain, none
BACKCOUNTRY CAMPSITE: none
SEASON: spring, summer, fall
MAP: USGS 7.5-minute Grand Lake

In the scenic Kawuneeche Valley, at the foot of the Never Summer Range, the rustic cabins of the Never Summer Ranch remain just as they did a century ago. A trip to this turn-of-the-century dude ranch makes a fascinating and scenic walk.

   The Never Summer Ranch is located on US Highway 34, 7.8 miles north of the Grand Lake Entrance Station and 13.2 miles west of the Alpine Visitor Center. There is a parking lot and picnic area at the trailhead.

   From the parking area, a dirt road crosses the Colorado River and travels a level 0.5 mile to the Never Summer Ranch. Easily managed by wheelchairs and strollers, this road provides a pleasant walk through the wide Kawuneeche Valley, through which the Colorado River flows for almost 7 miles. At the cluster of cabins that make up the ranch, bring out your guide, "Never Summer Ranch" (available at park visitor centers), and take yourself on a self-guided tour of the site. Open for your inspection are kitchens, bunkhouses, a taxidermy shop, old sleds, wagons, and more. The ranch reveals the rugged simplicity of dude ranching in the 1920s, when the West was still young. During the summer, park rangers lead entertaining interpretive walks to the ranch. Check at a park visitor center for schedules.

Visitors owe the preservation of this portion of the Kawuneeche Valley to the generosity of John Holzwarth, the former owner of the Never Summer Ranch. Before the ranch became part of the park, Holzwarth received numerous lucrative offers from speculators who wanted to build resorts on his property. Fortunately, Mr. Holzwarth declined these offers and earmarked the land for conservation. At age 71, he stated, "I can live with and die knowing that this valley will be for all and not a select few."

49

Kawuneeche Valley at Bowen/Baker Mountains

DIFFICULTY: nature stroll, handicapped access with
     assistance
DISTANCE: 0.5 mile one way
USAGE: low
STARTING ELEVATION: 8,864 feet; elevation gain, none
BACKCOUNTRY CAMPSITE: none
SEASON: spring, summer, fall
MAP: USGS 7.5-minute Grand Lake

This trip follows an unpaved road 0.5 mile through the wide and scenic Kawuneeche Valley. The level road, closed to vehicular traffic, gives every hiker, even those in wheelchairs, the opportunity to travel through the wide river valley, away from paved

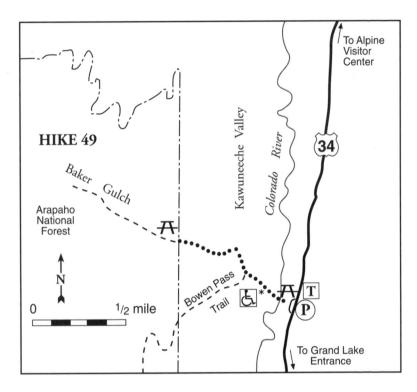

surfaces. Although the scenery is not spectacular, the valley views are still very fine, and the trail is usually uncrowded. At dawn or dusk look for deer or elk.

The Bowen/Baker Trailhead is located on the west side of US Highway 34, 6.4 miles north of the Grand Lake Entrance Station and 14.6 miles southwest of the Alpine Visitor Center. There is a parking lot and picnic area at the trailhead.

The old road starts out at the end of the picnic area and heads directly west across the valley. Enjoy a fine view of the Never Summer Range and the 7-mile-long Kawuneeche Valley, through which the North Fork of the Colorado leisurely courses. The pyramid-shaped peak to the west is Baker Mountain (12,397 feet). At the west end of the valley, the road divides. Take the fork on the right, leading to the Baker Gulch Trail.

After circling around a cabin, the road continues into a forest of lodgepole pine and aspen. A hike in the autumn amidst the aspen's golden fall foliage is recommended. Since this trailhead is not heavily used, the walk is quiet and lovely. The sounds of birds and squirrels can be clearly heard. After a half mile, the road ends (at the start of the Baker Gulch Trail and Arapaho National Forest). Secluded picnic tables are at the end of this road.

50

Coyote Valley Nature Trail

DIFFICULTY: self-guided nature stroll, handicapped
    accessible according to federal accessibility
    standards
DISTANCE: 1-mile loop
USAGE: low
STARTING ELEVATION: 8,766 feet; elevation gain, none
BACKCOUNTRY CAMPSITE: none
SEASON: spring, summer, fall
MAP: USGS 7.5-minute Grand Lake

This charming 1-mile loop trail offers superbly easy access to a wonderfully scenic and educational trail. Set on the edge of the Kawuneeche Valley, the level path parallels the Colorado River, enabling those with wheelchairs and strollers to enjoy a beautiful part of the park. Come early in the morning or at dusk to view a wide variety of wildlife. At any time, enjoy a picnic on tables at the meadow's edge.

    The Coyote Valley Trail is located 5.4 miles north of the Grand Lake Entrance Station and 2.3 miles south of the Timber Creek Campground.

    The trail begins in an old fir-spruce forest. Just opposite the trailhead sign, find an Engelmann spruce over 200 years old. A few yards down the trail to the right, an even larger spruce is estimated to be over 300. As you walk this new trail through this ancient valley, consider the changes these trees have witnessed.

    Cross the Colorado River over a stone bridge, and then turn right for the nature trail. Straight ahead a picnic area loops beneath the pines. Stroll slowly; this trail was built for comfort and contemplation. Waysides provide benches and interpretive signs every 200 to 400 feet.

The Coyote Valley Trail is named for the broad valley through which it travels. Just before this park was created, elders of the Arapaho tribe were asked to recount the ancient names given to the land. They called this valley *Kawuneeche,* meaning "valley of the coyotes." Today, coyotes can still be spotted in the meadow hunting small rodents and grasshoppers, and their calls are frequently heard at night. Look for their scat on the trail. Its shape is doglike, but its telltale sign is the presence of undigested fur.

This valley was once a rich gathering and hunting ground for the Arapaho. Many of the plants they picked for food and medicine remain. White and purple penstamen, wild parsley,

Looking for elk on the Coyote Nature Trail

yarrow, yellow sulfur flower, and pink pussy toes are just a few. The willow that lines the riverbanks supplied supple weaving materials as well as analgesic from its bark. Lodgepole pine (a grove is just ahead) provided narrow and lightweight poles for tepees.

Colorado cutthroat trout once thrived in the Colorado River, whose headwaters lie just 14 miles north at La Poudre Pass. Unfortunately, a water diversion project, the Grand Ditch, diverted about half of the river's volume, severely affecting fish habitat by reducing water flow and increasing the river's temperature. Observe the ditch by looking northwest to the eastern slope of the Never Summer Range, where a horizontal line scars the slope (easily spotted because of the erosion it generated). The Kawuneeche Valley is still a gorgeous place to fish, but anglers will find it challenging.

Time has not been so hard on the mammalian population here. The old fir-spruce forest east of the river remains home to porcupine, weasel, pine marten, and chickaree. In the heat of day, elk also seek refuge in the forest. Along the river, recently introduced moose may be found. Most dramatically in the spring, early summer, and fall, large elk herds graze the meadow. The valley is a prime viewing spot for the elk's mating rut in the fall. Visit between September 1 and mid-October, at about 45 minutes before dusk, to hear and see this unforgettable spectacle. There are few sights as stirring as watching elk run through the golden meadow against the superb backdrop of the snowcapped Never Summer Mountains.

Proceed down the path, passing a pond on the right, where children can search for minnows or tadpoles. Confirmed inhabitants of the pond include fairy shrimp and midges. Continue following the path as it loops through a grove of lodgepole pines at 0.5 mile from the trailhead. At the north end of the trail, pause at a viewpoint to appreciate the majestic peak of Baker Mountain (12,397 feet) rising behind beautiful Green Knoll. Some hikers may want to continue beyond the established trail to explore the area north along the river. Using the river as your guide, it is impossible to lose your way.

Those who wish to remain on the trail can take their time ambling back to the trailhead.

—————— 51 ——————

Green Mountain Loop

DIFFICULTY: strenuous
DISTANCE: 7-mile loop
USAGE: low
STARTING ELEVATION: 8,794 feet; elevation gain,
    858 feet
BACKCOUNTRY CAMPSITE: 2.4, 2.8, 2.9, and 5.1 miles
    from the trailhead
SEASON: summer, fall
MAP: USGS 7.5-minute Grand Lake

This long, uncrowded walk through a shady coniferous forest features an aspen grove, numerous creeks, a flowered meadow, and the scant remains of a nineteenth-century ranch. Although some visitors may find the miles through dense pines monotonous, this hike has a feeling of isolation that is not found on the park's more visited trails. Backpackers can find shady and secluded campsites along Onahu Creek, about 2.5 miles from the trailhead, and at Big Meadows, about 5.1 miles from the Onahu Creek Trailhead but only 1.9 miles from the Green Mountain Trailhead.

Drop hikers off at the Onahu Creek Trailhead, located on the east side of US Highway 34, 3.2 miles north of the Grand Lake Entrance Station and 17.8 miles southwest of the Alpine Visitor Center. Park at the Green Mountain Trailhead, located 0.6 mile south of the Onahu Creek Trailhead on US Highway 34, and then rejoin your group by walking north along the highway or on a path parallel to the highway. Find this path by continuing due north shortly after the sign for the Green Mountain Trailhead.

The trail begins among aspen trees that have been liberally grazed by elk, which eat the bark when other food is scarce. Bulls eat the bark in the fall and winter, while cows seem to do so in the winter and spring. The bark may have some coagulative properties that aid the cows in their birthing season.

Soon after leaving the aspens, enter a dense and extensive "doghair" stand of lodgepole pines. Although these trees are spindly pole timber, they are probably 70 to 150 years old. Lodgepole

"Dog hair" forest on Onahu Creek Trail

pine forests often have a large number of toppled trees because their root systems are shallow, making them vulnerable to what foresters call "windthrow," the uprooting of trees by wind. Fallen trees remain on the ground for a long time because the rate of decomposition is slow at this altitude, where soils are too cold for many of the organisms that aid in decomposition.

Along this portion of the trail, children can play an alphabet game by finding letters in the configurations made by the fallen trees. A second trail game is mental "pick up sticks," in which children look at a maze of uprooted trees and try to figure out which tree could be removed without tumbling the pile.

As you progress up the trail, young firs and spruce appear. These trees represent the next stage in the forest succession. As they grow, they will shade out, and thus eventually kill, the sun-loving lodgepole pines. Notice also the rocky mountain junipers, whose berries smell like gin when crushed. Growing on the forest floor is broom huckleberry, providing a green shag carpet and sweet berries.

Listen for the sound of red squirrels, or chickarees, which chatter angrily in the trees overhead. Finding one is difficult, however, because the squirrels are skilled ventriloquists. Look for their nests, made of twigs and leaves and placed high in fir trees. Listen also for the mountain chickadee, which calls out its name over and over.

At 2.2 miles from the trailhead, the trail levels out and follows Onahu Creek. Walking along the bubbling creek is a pleasant change. Big rocks by the creek and a series of bridges make nice picnic spots. In this area there are three campsites, located 2.4 to 2.9 miles from the Onahu Creek Trailhead.

After crossing the last bridge over Onahu Creek at 2.9 miles, arrive at the junction with the Timber Creek Trail. Bear right (south) on this trail; signs at the junction clearly mark the way. This portion of the trail traverses a north-facing slope through a mature forest of Engelmann spruce and subalpine fir. As the trail climbs higher, the lodgepoles return. After 1.2 miles, arrive at the junction with the Tonahutu Creek Trail, which enters from the east. Proceed south (right) on the Tonahutu Creek Trail to Big Meadows.

The 0.7-mile walk along the edge of Big Meadows is very pleasant. The wide meadow is filled with wildflowers and long grasses. Wild strawberries grow by the trail and bear fruit in late summer. Deer and elk tracks can be seen. Toward the south end of the meadow are the scant remains of the ranch of Sam Stone, including his cabin and barn. In the early 1900s, Sam Stone attempted to grow hay in this meadow. Despite his lack of success at farming, he must have been cheered by the beautiful view out his door.

Near the south end of the meadow is the Big Meadows campsite, 5.1 miles from the Onahu Creek Trailhead. This campsite is an excellent and easy backpacking destination when approached from the Green Mountain Trailhead, only 1.9 miles away (see Hike 52).

At the end of the meadow, the Green Mountain Trail comes in from the west to join the Tonahutu Creek Trail. Bear right (southwest) at this junction, 1.6 miles from the Green Mountain Trailhead. Once again, the trail is well marked.

This is the last leg of the loop. The trail passes a second, smaller meadow frequented by deer and follows a small musical brook all the way back to the Green Mountain Trailhead.

HIKING OPTION:

Across the road from the Onahu Creek Trailhead, and 0.1 mile north, is a fisherman's trail leading to a series of large beaver dams and lodges along the Colorado River.

52

Big Meadows

DIFFICULTY: easy
DISTANCE: 1.8 miles one way
USAGE: low
STARTING ELEVATION: 8,794 feet; elevation gain,
     606 feet
BACKCOUNTRY CAMPSITE: 1.9 miles from the trailhead
SEASON: summer, fall
MAP: USGS 7.5-minute Grand Lake

This is a short hike through subalpine forest to a pretty, flowered meadow by the ruins of an early settler's ranch. The trail was originally the wagon road to the ranch, and to this day the path remains wide and smooth. At dawn or dusk there is a good chance of seeing deer. The meadow is also a superb place to view the rut of the elk in the late fall. Backpackers will find an excellent campsite at the meadow, just 1.9 miles from the trailhead.

Drive to the Green Mountain Trailhead, as described in Hike 51. There is a parking lot at the trailhead. A musical brook accompanies the trail to the meadow. Look for the tasty ground

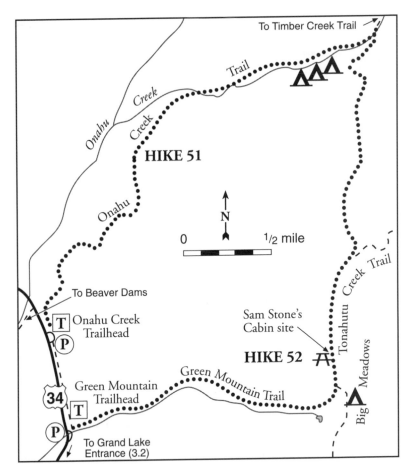

cover of wild blueberries and the less abundant, but equally delicious, wild strawberries. Feel free to sample, but remember that it is against park regulations to carry out more than a small quantity of edibles for your own consumption. It is best just to taste, and leave the rest for the next hikers or the park's wildlife.

The trail climbs moderately to Big Meadows, passing two small wet meadows along the way. Look for deer in these openings, especially very early or late in the day. Listen for the pleasant chirping of mountain chickadees and the angry scolding of the chickarees, or red squirrels.

Big Meadows, 1.8 uphill miles from the trailhead, is a large, open meadow that provides welcome change from the shady trail. Many wildflowers grow amid the grass. Look for shrubby cinquefoil, a five-petaled yellow flower. Native Americans and early settlers discovered many valuable uses for this member of the rose family. The roots dry beautifully and are reputed to taste like sweet potatoes. Other parts of this plant were used to treat stomach ailments, fevers, toothaches, and infections. Look also for pink elephantheads, which mimic tiny elephant heads with upturned trunks and floppy ears. A herd of heads is arranged vertically on each stalk.

The trail leads to the remains of two log structures, the cabin and barn of Sam Stone, who attempted to harvest hay here in the early 1900s. You walked up his pleasant wagon road to arrive at this meadow. After toiling for years at his largely unsuccessful hay operation, he left this site to prospect, unsuccessfully, for gold.

This is a great spot for a picnic. Golden-mantled ground squirrels and chipmunks come for lunch, but resist feeding them. It's easy to tell the difference between the ground squirrel and a chipmunk. The golden-mantled ground squirrel is much larger and has stripes only on its sides. The chipmunk has stripes on its back and on its face. In addition, the chipmunk is quicker and more nervous, rarely sitting still for more than a moment.

Watch also for the fluffy-headed gray jay, a common resident of the subalpine forest. The gray jay is slightly larger than a robin and is primarily gray, with white markings on its forehead and neck, and black on the back of its head. You may also spot a weasel on its almost constant hunt for prey. To fuel its long, tubular body, the weasel must eat an amount equal to two-thirds of its body weight per day. Hunger and instinct drive this intrepid predator to attack animals up to thirty times its size. Look also for deer and elk tracks on the trail; the animals themselves are not likely to appear here in midday.

At the south end of the meadow, 1.9 miles from the Green Mountain Trailhead, is a campsite that would make an excellent destination for a family backpacking trip. A night at this site would simulate Sam Stone's experience of almost a century ago. Stories about prospectors, Indians, or early settlers would greatly enrich the experience for children. (See appendix C.)

Sam Stone's cabin at Big Meadows

After exploring Big Meadows, retrace your steps, this time all downhill, back to the Green Mountain Trailhead.

HIKING OPTIONS:
This trail is one section of the Green Mountain Loop Trail, described in Hike 51.

53

North Inlet Meadow

DIFFICULTY: nature stroll, handicapped access with
       assistance
DISTANCE: 1.2 miles one way
USAGE: moderate
STARTING ELEVATION: 8,540 feet; elevation gain, none
BACKCOUNTRY CAMPSITE: 1.2 miles from the trailhead
SEASON: spring, summer, fall
MAP: USGS 7.5-minute Grand Lake

This hike heads down an unpaved road to a meadow popular with campers and picnickers. Summerland Park, only 1.2 miles from the trailhead, is a short and easy destination for backpacking families.

Drive to the Tonahutu/North Inlet trailhead. From US Highway 34 in Grand Lake, turn east onto Colorado State Highway 278. After 0.3 mile, come to a fork. Keep left, and drive 0.8 mile to a dirt road. Turn left again and follow this road past a parking lot, up a hill, and over Tonahutu Creek. The parking lot for the Tonahutu/North Inlet Trailhead is just after the bridge.

The hike begins at the east end of the parking lot and follows the dirt road, which is closed to traffic. The gently rolling road is easy to walk, although it may be wet and muddy in places. The road, which borders private ranchland, passes flowered meadows with grazing horses and cows, set against a background of rocky peaks. It feels like a stroll down a fine country road.

After 1.2 gentle miles, reach sunny Summerland Park, which is usually populated with tents and picnickers. Summerland Park is a very easy backpacking destination and is a good place for a summer lunch. There is plenty of open space for children to explore. An accessible stream flows along the southern edge of the park.

54

Cascade Falls

DIFFICULTY: strenuous
DISTANCE: 3.5 miles one way
USAGE: moderate
STARTING ELEVATION: 8,540 feet; elevation gain,
     300 feet
BACKCOUNTRY CAMPSITE: 1, 2, 3, and 3.5 miles from
     the trailhead
SEASON: summer, fall
MAP: USGS 7.5-minute Grand Lake

Cascade Falls is a wide, raucous, magnificent waterfall. The trail is a long but easy walk along a sunny, unpaved road and then through moist, shady subalpine forest. The falls are an excellent destination for a picnic.

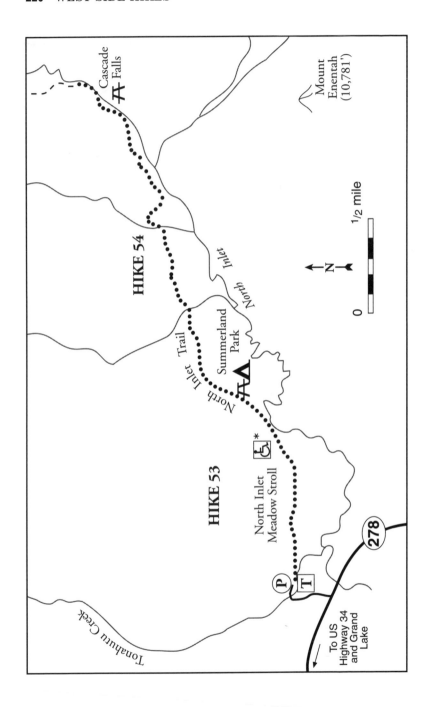

Walk to Summerland Park, as described in Hike 53. Beyond the sunny, often crowded park, the mostly level trail enters a forest of lodgepole pine and aspen. Eventually, the lodgepole forest gives way to subalpine fir and Engelmann spruce.

The valley increasingly narrows, and the walls of the mountains rise more steeply on each side. The cliffs are beautiful, dripping with moss, glowing wet from this area's frequent summer rainstorms. A variety of moisture-loving wildflowers thrives beside the trail.

At 3.5 miles from the trailhead, arrive at Cascade Falls, where the sound of crashing water drowns out any conversation. There is good exploring and rock scrambling both above and below the falls. Vantage points above and below offer unique perspectives of the wide torrent. Children need to be closely supervised when approaching the falls, for wet, mossy rocks are slippery. The large flat rocks above the falls provide superior places to picnic.

55

Adams Falls

DIFFICULTY: easy
DISTANCE: 0.3 mile one way
USAGE: high
STARTING ELEVATION: 8,391 feet; elevation gain, 79 feet
BACKCOUNTRY CAMPSITE: none
SEASON: summer, fall
MAP: USGS 7.5-minute Shadow Mountain

A very short walk leads to one of the most magnificent waterfalls in the park. Get an early start to avoid the crowds. Early morning hikers may also be rewarded with a sparkling rainbow made by the rising sun shining through the falls.

The East Inlet Trailhead is located near the West Portal of the Adams Tunnel. From US Highway 34 in Grand Lake, turn east on Colorado State Highway 278. After a third of a mile, the highway divides; take the road to the left which leads away from the village, and drive 2.1 miles to a large parking lot. The trailhead is at the east end of the lot.

View over Adams Falls

The wide path to the falls is lined with lodgepole pines and aspens. The trail heads uphill moderately, so for the smallest hikers the short distance to the falls is a blessing. This hike is a good one for children because most motivated youngsters over age four can walk the entire distance. Reaching the falls without the aid of an adult should bring great pride to a young hiker.

Adams Falls is impressive and imposing. Torrents of water tumble down a wide gully, then rush into a narrow canyon with tall rock walls. The power of the water is felt in the rising spray and the thundering sound of the water sweeping over the rocks.

Explore the area around the falls, but supervise children carefully. The wet rocks are slick and can be dangerous.

HIKING OPTION:

A good addition to this short hike is to continue east beyond the falls to a series of scenic meadows, 1.4 miles away (see Hike 56).

56

East Inlet Meadows Trail

DIFFICULTY: easy
DISTANCE: 1.7 miles one way
USAGE: low
STARTING ELEVATION: 8,391 feet; elevation gain, 159 feet
BACKCOUNTRY CAMPSITE: 1.5 miles from the trailhead
SEASON: summer, fall
MAP: USGS 7.5-minute Shadow Mountain

This pleasant, nearly level walk leads to magnificent Adams Falls and beyond to a series of meadows rimmed by mountains. The scenery has a gentle beauty that is enhanced by the solitude of the uncrowded trail. There is plenty of opportunity to explore the meandering East Inlet as it winds through the meadows and to

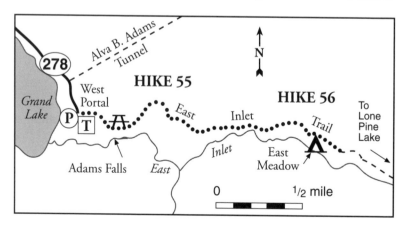

look for beavers and muskrats along its banks. A superb back-country campsite is an easy 1.5-mile hike from the trailhead.

Drive to the East Inlet Trailhead and hike to Adams Falls, as described in Hike 55. During the short, steep climb to the falls, you gain more than half of the total altitude gained on this hike. After enjoying the truly impressive waterfall, continue east on the trail, following the East Inlet. This river is one of two water courses that flow down from the Continental Divide into Grand Lake. The other river, to the north, is called North Inlet.

The river above the falls is lively and noisy. The path follows the river through a shady forest of lodgepole pines and aspens. Large rocks line the trail, some in interesting formations. To the left of the trail, look for an aspen tree tenaciously growing from the scant soil on top of a boulder. Aspens can grow in areas that are too rocky, wet, or infertile for other trees.

Aspens are easily identified by their small, trembling leaves and whitish-gray bark. They are one of the few deciduous trees found in the Rocky Mountains, but they are widespread and abundant in the range. In the fall, aspens turn brilliant yellow or orange, providing a dramatic contrast to the deep greens of the more abundant conifers. Aspens are usually found in disturbed areas, including places that have recently burned, been logged, or have been subjected to avalanches or rock slides.

The smallest puff of wind causes aspen leaves to tremble. The quaking aspen's scientific name, *Populus tremuloides*, reflects this trembling motion. The quaking is caused by the way the leaf is attached to its long slender stem. An early missionary to the north country recorded that superstitious woodsmen believed that Jesus was crucified on a cross made out of aspen and that the tree has been trembling ever since.

Approximately 1.3 miles from the trailhead, arrive at the first of two meadows. The view is lovely across the meadow. At the east end stands Mount Craig, or Mount Baldy, as it is commonly called in Grand Lake. This impressive 12,007-foot mountain is well named, for it has, in fact, a treeless rock dome for a summit. A variety of wildflowers grow by the river, which is easily reached by spur trails.

You can spend time at this small meadow or continue to East Meadow, a larger meadow, 0.5 mile farther down the trail. Right before reaching East Meadow a sign announces the East Meadow Campsite. This site, 1.5 miles from the trailhead, is an easy back-

Mount Craig (Mount Baldy) from East Inlet Trail

packing destination for a young family. The meadow is an exquisite, uncrowded place to camp.

As at the first meadow, Mount Baldy presides over East
Meadow. The East Inlet snakes through the meadow in horseshoe
curves. Spur trails lead to the water. There are signs of beaver
activity along the river, so look carefully for lodges and dams.
During the day, you are unlikely to see a beaver because they are
usually active after dusk. Watch for them if you are camping at
East Meadow or hiking very late in the day. Muskrats also frequent this habitat and may reside in abandoned beaver lodges.
At dusk watch for deer.

If you're not spending the night, take a leisurely walk to the
east side of the meadow. At its east end the trail starts to gain
altitude as it makes its way to Lone Pine Lake, 5.5 miles east. This
is a good place to turn around. In late summer, your walk back is
enhanced by snacks from wild raspberry bushes along the trail.

Appendixes

A. Hike Finder

Key to symbols:
Handicap access: (H) = Yes, according to uniform federal standards of accessibility; (H*) = Yes, with assistance
Mileage: RT = round trip; OW = one way
Difficulty: NS = Nature stroll; E = Easy; M = Moderate; S = Strenuous VS = Very Strenuous
Usage: L = Low; M = Moderate; H = High
Point of interest: G = Geological formation; NT = Nature trail (self-guided); P = Peak; H = Historical interest; I = Interpretive signs

	Difficulty	Mileage	Usage	Backpacking	Fishing	Scenic views	Fall foliage	Wildlife	Point of interest
EAST SIDE HIKES									
1. Arch Rocks and the Pool	E	1.5/1.7 OW	H	•	•			•	G
2. Cub Lake and the Pool Loop	M	2.3/6.0 OW	H	•	•			•	
3. Moraine Park (H*)	NS	0.25 OW	M						G
4. Mill Creek Basin	E	1.6 OW	M	•				•	H
5. Sprague Lake (H)	NS	0.5 OW	H	•	•			•	NT
6. Boulder Brook/Alberta Falls Loop	S	5.6 RT	L/H	•		•	•	•	
7. Alberta Falls	E	0.6 OW	H			•	•		
8. Mills Lake	M	2.5 OW	H			•	•	•	
9. The Loch	M	2.7 OW	H	•	•	•	•	•	
10. Timberline Falls, Lake of Glass, and Sky Pond	S	4.0/4.6 OW	M	•	•	•	•	•	
11. Bear Lake (H*)	NS	0.5 OW	H					•	NT
12. Nymph Lake	E	0.5 OW	H			•	•		
13. Dream Lake	E	1.1 OW	H		•	•	•		
14. Emerald Lake	M	1.8 OW	H			•	•	•	
15. Lake Haiyaha	M	2.1 OW	H		•	•	•	•	
16. Bierstadt Lake	E	1.7 OW	M			•	•		

	Difficulty	Mileage	Usage	Backpacking	Fishing	Scenic views	Fall foliage	Wildlife	Point of interest
17. Flattop Mountain	S	4.4 OW	H			•	•	•	P
18. Gem Lake	M	1.8/2.0 OW	H			•	•	•	G
19. Deserted Village	M	3.0 OW	L				•		P
20. Bridal Veil Falls	M	3.2 OW	L	•			•		G
21. Deer Mountain	S	3.0 OW	H			•			P
22. Alluvial Fan Trail (H*)	NS	0.5 OW	H						H
23. Beaver Boardwalk (H)	NS	0.25 RT	H					•	I
24. Mummy Range	S	1.5/3.5 OW	L			•		•	P
25. Lily Mountain	M	1.5 OW	M			•			P
26. Lily Lake (H)	NS	1.0 RT	M	•					
27. Eugenia Mine	E	1.4 OW	M	•					H
28. Estes Cone	S	3.3 OW	M	•		•			P
29. Chasm Lake	S	4.2 OW	H	•	•	•		•	
30. Longs Peak	VS	8.0 OW	H	•		•		•	P/H
31. Copeland Falls (H*)	NS	0.3 OW	H				•		
32. Calypso Cascades	E	1.8 OW	H	•			•		
33. Ouzel Falls	M	2.7 OW	H	•		•	•	•	
TRAIL RIDGE HIKES									
34. Indian Game Drive System Trail	E	0.75 OW	L			•		•	H
35. Upper Old Ute Trail	M	2.0 OW	M			•	•		H
36. Forest Canyon Overlook (H*)	NS	0.25 OW	H			•		•	I
37. Sundance Mountain	M	0.5 OW	L			•			P
38. Tundra Trail at Rock Cut (H*)	NS	0.5	H				•	•	G/I
39. Marmot Point	E	0.5 OW	M			•		•	P
40. Fall River Pass Tundra Trail	E	0.25 OW	H			•			I

	Difficulty	Mileage	Usage	Backpacking	Fishing	Scenic views	Fall foliage	Wildlife	Point of interest
41. Fall River Pass to Forest Canyon	E	1.9 OW	L			•		•	
42. Milner Pass to Forest Canyon Pass	M	2.3 OW	L			•		•	
43. Milner Pass along the Continental Divide	S	2.1 OW	L			•		•	
WEST SIDE HIKES									
44. Poudre River Trail	E	1.0/2.5 OW	L					•	
45. The Crater	M	1.0 OW	M			•		•	
46. Lulu City	M	3.6 OW	M		•		•	•	H
47. Grand Ditch	S	3.4 OW	L	•		•	•	•	H
48. Never Summer Ranch (H*)	NS	0.75 OW	H						H
49. Kawuneeche Valley at Bowen/Baker Mountains (H*)	NS	0.5 OW	L				•		
50. Coyote Valley Nature Trail (H)	NS	1.0 RT	L		•			•	I
51. Green Mountain Loop	S	7.0 RT	L	•					H
52. Big Meadows	E	1.8 OW	L	•				•	H
53. North Inlet Meadow (H*)	NS	1.2 OW	M	•					
54. Cascade Falls	S	3.5 OW	M	•					
55. Adams Falls	E	0.3 OW	H						
56. East Inlet Meadows Trail	E	1.7 OW	L	•	•		•	•	

B. Wildlife Locator Chart

TIME = Time of day most often seen. SEASON = Season of activity. Information supplied in part by NPS, RMNP.

ANIMAL	TIME	SEASON	HABITAT	LIKELY LOCATIONS AND TRAILS
Chipmunk	Day	Sp, Su, F	Open areas from forest to tundra	Abundant parkwide
Golden-mantled ground squirrel	Day	Sp, Su, F	Mixed and coniferous forest	Abundant parkwide
Abert's squirrel	Day	Sp, Su, F	Ponderosa woodland	East side at lower elevations; hikes 18, 25
Red squirrel (chickaree)	Day	Sp, Su, F	Dense forests of spruce and fir, Douglas fir, or lodgepole pine	Parkwide at lower elevations
Wyoming ground squirrel	Day	Sp, Su, F	Parks, open valleys, and meadows, 6,000–12,000 feet	Parkwide; hikes 3, 4
Pika	Day	Sp, Su, F	Talus slopes and rock outcrops near and above treeline	Parkwide at higher elevations; hikes 6–10, 14, 15, 17, 24, 29, 30, 34–43, 45, 47
Yellow-bellied marmot	Day	Sp, Su, F	Talus slopes and rock outcrops near and above treeline	Parkwide at higher elevations; hikes 6–10, 14, 15, 17, 24, 29–30, 34–43, 45, 47
Weasel (long-tailed weasel, short-tailed weasel)	Anytime	Year-round	Stream courses from forest to tundra, but generally under 10,000 feet	Parkwide; hikes 1, 2, 4, 6–24, 27, 28, 32, 42–44, 46, 47, 51–56

ANIMAL	TIME	SEASON	HABITAT	LIKELY LOCATIONS AND TRAILS
Beaver	Dusk, night	Sp, Su, F	Streams and ponds	Parkwide at lower elevations; hikes 1, 2, 23, 46, 51, 56
Porcupine	Anytime	Year-round	Pine woodlands and willow thickets	Parkwide at lower elevations; hikes 1, 2, 46, 51, 52, 56
Coyote	Anytime, but especially at dawn and dusk	Year-round	Open areas	Parkwide, especially at Horseshoe Park, Moraine Park, Beaver Meadows, Upper Poudre River, Upper Kawuneeche Valley
Black bear	Dusk	Sp, Su, F	Forests	Parkwide, though very few in park
River otter	Anytime	Year-round	Streams, ponds	Lower Kawuneeche Valley
Mule deer	Dawn, dusk	Year-round	Brushy areas, meadow and forest edges; in summer, on alpine tundra near willow thickets or *krummholz*	Abundant parkwide, especially Moraine Park, Trail Ridge Road, Endovalley, Horseshoe Park, Upper Kawuneeche Valley; hikes 1, 2, 24, 34–46
Elk (wapiti)	Dawn	Year-round	Summer: alpine meadows, tundra *krummholz* woodland, forest edges. Fall, winter, spring: lower montane woodland, montane meadows	Summer: parkwide at higher elevations; Trail Ridge Road, Gore Range Overlook, Upper Old Fall River Road (Willow Park, Chapin Pass); hikes 34–43. Fall, winter, spring: at lower elevations; Horseshoe Park, Beaver Meadows, Moraine Park, Kawuneeche Valley, Big Meadows

ANIMAL	TIME	SEASON	HABITAT	LIKELY LOCATIONS AND TRAILS
Bighorn sheep	Day	Year-round	Alpine meadows near rocky cliffs	Sheep Lakes at Horseshoe Park; hikes 24, 42, 43, 45
Moose	Anytime	Year-round	Willow thickets, lodgepole forests	Very few in park; Kawuneeche Valley; hikes 46–52
Mallard	Day	Sp, Su, F	Lakes, streams, ponds	Parkwide at lower elevations; hikes 2, 5, 8, 9, 11–13, 16, 23, 46, 56
Hairy Woodpecker	Day	Year-round	Montane forests, river groves, and mixed forests	Abundant parkwide; hikes 1, 2, 18, 31–33
Red-tailed hawk	Day, especially midday	Sp, Su, F	Open country, areas with high rock ledges and adjacent woodland	Open meadows of lower and middle elevations, Lumpy Ridge; hikes 4, 1–8, 21
White-tailed ptarmigan	Day	Year-round	Alpine tundra	Parkwide on tundra; hikes 17, 24, 34–43, 45

C. Taking Your Experience Home: Recommended Reading

The books and periodicals listed below promote an understanding, appreciation, and respect for the environment. Through reading, children can build upon their park experiences and prepare for their next outdoor adventure.

The Rocky Mountain Nature Association is a good source of books about the Rocky Mountains. The Association runs book concessions at park visitor centers and the Moraine Park Museum. Proceeds from sales benefit park educational programs. For a free mail-order catalog, write the Rocky Mountain Nature Association, Rocky Mountain National Park, Estes Park, CO 80517, or call (970) 586-1258.

The following organizations also offer excellent nature books on a wide variety of topics:
• National Wildlife Federation, 1400 16th Street Northwest, Washington, D.C. 20036, 1-800-432-4564.
• National Geographic Society, Educational Services, Washington, D.C. 20036, 1-800-368-2728.
• The Sierra Club, 730 Polk Street, San Francisco, CA 94109, (415) 923-5500.

BOOKS FOR CHILDREN
Field Guides
Alden, Peter. *Mammals—A Simplified Field Guide to the Common Mammals of North America*. Boston: Houghton Mifflin Co., 1987.

Arnosky, Jim. *Secrets of a Wildlife Watcher—A Beginner Field Guide*. New York: Beech Tree Books, 1991.

Jones, Charlotte Foltz. *Colorado Wildflowers: A Beginner's Field Guide*. Helena, MT: Falcon Press, 1994.

Peterson, Roger Tory. *Birds—Simplified Field Guide*. Boston: Houghton Mifflin Co., 1986.

Seacrest, Betty R. *Rocky Mountain Birds—Easy Identification*. Boulder, CO: Avery Press, 1993.

Stall, Chris. *Animal Tracks of the Rocky Mountains*. Seattle: The Mountaineers, 1989.

Watts, Tom. *Rocky Mountain Treefinder*. Nature Study Guild, 1972.

Games and Activities

Kreider, Elizabeth. *High Country Games—An Environmental Activity Book*. Estes Park, CO: Rocky Mountain Nature Association, 1984.

Larson, Helen Henkel. *Rocky Mountain National Park Coloring Book*. Eureka, CA: Earthwalk Press, 1993.

Peterson, Roger Tory and Peter Alden. *A Field Guide to Mammals Coloring Book*. Boston: Houghton Mifflin Co., 1987.

Peterson, Roger Tory and Frances Tenenbaum. *A Field Guide to Wildflowers Coloring Book*. Boston: Houghton Mifflin Co., 1982.

General Nonfiction

Cooper, Ann. *Above the Treeline*. Denver: Denver Museum of Natural History Press, 1996.

———. *In the Forest*. Denver: Denver Museum of Natural History Press, 1996.

Cornell, Joseph Dharat. *Journey to the Heart of Nature*. Nevada City, CA: Dawn Publications, 1994.

The Earthworks Group. *50 Simple Things Kids Can Do to Save the Earth*. New York: Universal Press Syndicate, 1990.

Evans, Lisa Gollin. *An Elephant Never Forgets Its Snorkel*. New York: Crown Books for Young Readers, Inc., 1992.

Freedman, Russell. *Buffalo Hunt*. New York: Holiday House, 1988.

Gilmore, Jack. *Year at Elk Meadow*. Boulder, CO: Roberts Rinehart, Inc., 1986.

Haluska, Vicky. *The Arapaho Indians*. New York: Chelsea House Publishers, 1993.

Hirshi, Ron. *Headgear*. New York: Dodd, Mead and Company, 1986.

Parker, Steve. *Pond and River*. New York: Alfred A. Knopf, 1988.

Pettit, Jan. *Utes: The Mountain People*. Boulder, CO: Johnson Books, 1990.

Robertson, Kayo. *Signs Along the River—Learning to Read the Natural Landscape*. Boulder, CO: Roberts Rinehart, Inc., 1986.

Smith, Lucy. *Improve Your Survival Skills*. Tulsa, OK: Usborne EDC Publishing, Inc., 1996.

Picture Books

Aronsky, Jim. *Come Out, Muskrat*. New York: Lothrop, Lee and Shepard, 1989.

———. *Deer at the Brook*. New York: Lothrop, Lee and Shepard, 1986.

Donahue, Mike. *The Grandpa Tree*. Boulder, CO: Roberts Rinehart, Inc., 1988.

George, Jean Craighead. *One Day in the Alpine Tundra*. New York: Thomas Y. Crowell, 1984.

———. *One Day in the Woods*. New York: Thomas Y. Crowell, 1988.

Plumb, Sally. *A Pika's Tail*. Jackson, WY: Grand Teton Natural History Association, 1994.

Steptoe, John. *The Story of Jumping Mouse*. New York: Mulberry Books, 1984.

Fiction

Connolly, James E., ed. *Why the Possum's Tail is Bare and Other North American Nature Tales*. Owings Mills, MD: Stemmer House, 1985.

George, Jean Craighead. *Julie of the Wolves*. New York: Harper & Row, 1972.

———. *My Side of the Mountain*. New York: E. P. Dutton, 1975.

Mowat, Farley. *Never Cry Wolf*. Boston: Little, Brown and Company, 1963.

Rawlings, Marjorie Kinnan. *The Yearling*. New York: Collier Macmillan Publishers, 1938.

Savage, Deborah. *A Rumour of Otters*. Boston: Houghton Mifflin Co., 1986.

Seuss, Dr. *The Lorax*. New York: Random House, 1971.

Periodicals

National Geographic World. National Geographic Society, Washington, D.C. 20036. Ages 8-14.

Ranger Rick. National Wildlife Federation. Ages 6-12.

Your Big Backyard. National Wildlife Federation. Ages 3-5.

Zoobooks. Wildlife Education Ltd., P.O. Box 28870, San Diego, CA 92128. Ages 1-12.

BOOKS FOR PARENTS

Sharing Nature with Children

Brown, Tom, Jr. with Judy Brown. *Tom Brown's Field Guide to Nature and Survival for Children*. New York: Berkley Publishing Group, 1989.

Caduto, Michael J. and Joseph Bruchac. *Keepers of the Earth: Native American Stories and Environmental Activities for Children*. Golden, CO: Fulcrum, Inc., 1989.

———. *Keepers of the Night: Native American Stories and Noctural Activities for Children*. Golden, CO: Fulcrum, Inc., 1994.

Carson, Rachel. *The Sense of Wonder*. New York: Harper & Row, 1984.

Cornell, Joseph Bharat. *Sharing Nature with Children*. Nevada City, CA: Dawn Publications, 1979.

Ross, Micheal Elsohn. *The Happy Camper Handbook*. Yosemite National Park, CA: Yosemite National Park, 1995.

First-Aid Books

Brown, Robert E. *Emergency Survival Handbook*. Bellevue, WA: American Outdoor Safety League, 1987.

Carline, Jan D., Martha J. Lentz, and Steven C. Macdonald. *Mountaineering First Aid*. Seattle: The Mountaineers, 1996.

Natural History

Armstrong, David M. *Rocky Mountain Mammals*. Boulder, CO: Colorado Associated University Press, 1982.

Buccholtz, C. W. *Rocky Mountain Park: A History*. Boulder, CO: Colorado Associated University Press, 1983.

Cutts, Gretchen S. *Potions, Portions, Poisons: Indian and Settler Plant Uses*. Estes Park, CO: Rocky Mountain Nature Association, 1985.

Dannen, Kent and Donna Dannen. *Rocky Mountain National Park Hiking Trails*. Old Saybrook, CT: Globe Pequot Press, 1994.

———. *Rocky Mountain Wildflowers*. Estes Park, CO: Tundra Publications, 1981.

———. *Walks with Nature in Rocky Mountain National Park*.

Charlotte, NC: The East Woods Press, 1981.

Gray, Mary Taylor. *Watchable Birds of the Rocky Mountains*. Missoula, MT: Mountain Press Publishing Co., 1992.

Rezendes, Paul. *Track and the Art of Seeing*. Charlotte, VT: Camden House Publishing, Inc., 1992.

Peterson, Roger Tory. *A Field Guide to Western Birds*. Boston: Houghton Mifflin Co., 1961.

Shattil, Wendy, Bob Rozinski, and Budd Titlow. *Rocky Mountain National Park: Beyond Trail Ridge*. Englewood, CO: Westcliffe Publishers, Inc., 1986.

Torbit, Stephen C. *Large Mammals of the Central Rockies*. Monte Vista, CA: Bennet Creek Publications, 1987.

Whitney, Stephen. *Western Forests*. New York: Alfred A. Knopf, 1985.

Willard, Beatrice and Michael T. Smithson. *Alpine Wildflowers of the Rocky Mountains*. Estes Park, CO: Rocky Mountain Nature Association, n.d.

Zwinger, Ann. *Beyond the Aspen Grove*. New York: Random House, 1970.

Zwinger, Ann and Beatrice Willard. *Land Above the Trees*. New York: Harper & Row, 1972.

Index

About the Author

Lisa Gollin Evans received her B.A. from Cornell University, then obtained a J.D. from Boalt Hall School of Law. Between books Evans works in the field of environmental law, most recently for the Massachusetts Department of Coastal Zone Management.

Evans believes the best way to create tomorrow's environmentalists is to expose children to the wonders, beauty, and excitement of nature. Her books include *Lake Tahoe: A Family Guide, An Outdoor Family Guide to Acadia National Park,* and *An Outdoor Family Guide to Yellowstone and Grand Teton National Parks.* She has also written a nonfiction book for children, *An Elephant Never Forgets Its Snorkel,* which was named an "outstanding science book for children" in 1992 by the National Association of Teachers and the Children's Book Council. Evans lives with her husband and three daughters in Marblehead, Massachusetts.

Founded in 1906, The Mountaineers is a Seattle-based non-profit outdoor activity and conservation club with 15,000 members, whose mission is "to explore, study, preserve, and enjoy the natural beauty of the outdoors . . . . " The club sponsors many classes and year-round outdoor activities in the Pacific Northwest, and supports environmental causes by sponsoring legislation and presenting educational programs. The Mountaineers Books supports the club's mission by publishing travel and natural history guides, instructional texts, and works on conservation and history. For information, call or write The Mountaineers, Club Headquarters, 300 Third Avenue West, Seattle, Washington, 98119; (206) 284-6310.

Send or call for our catalog of more than 300 outdoor titles:

The Mountaineers Books
1001 SW Klickitat Way, Suite 201
Seattle, WA 98134
1-800-553-4453
e-mail: mbooks@mountaineers.org
website: www.mountaineers.org